THE GOURMET
Mexican Kitchen
A COOKBOOK

Bold Flavors FOR THE HOME CHEF

Shannon Bard

CHEF/OWNER OF ZAPOTECA RESTAURANT AND TEQUILERIA AND
MIXTECA TAQUERIA AND CANTINA

PAGE STREET
PUBLISHING CO.

PAGE STREET
PUBLISHING CO.

First published in 2015 by

Page Street Publishing Co.

27 Congress Street, Suite 103

Salem, MA 01970

www.pagestreetpublishing.com

Distributed by Macmillan; sales in Canada by The Canadian Manda Group; distribution in Canada by The Jaguar Book Group.

18   17   16   15   1   2   3   4   5

ISBN-13: 978-1-62414-096-9

ISBN-10: 1-62414-096-3

Library of Congress Control Number: 2014948996

Cover and book design by Page Street Publishing Co.

Photography by Ted Axelrod

Printed and bound in China

Page Street is proud to be a member of 1% for the Planet. Members donate one percent of their sales to one or more of the over 1,500 environmental and sustainability charities across the globe who participate in this program.

In Memory

MY MOTHER AND GRANDMOTHERS

Who taught me a love of cooking that has now become my passion.

Dedication

TOM—MY LOVE, HUSBAND AND BEST FRIEND

For believing in me despite all odds as well as for a million other things.

DYLAN, DEVIN, LOGAN & CAMDEN

For being you. My hope is to make you proud and be an example
that it is never too late to follow your dreams.

Introducción

INTRODUCTION

In my family, we love to cook. Somehow cooking has always been something that created a happy experience for me, even before I became a professional chef. Maybe it was because the resulting meals would be enjoyed with my family sitting around our large kitchen table, appreciating not only what I prepared but also each other's company. Or maybe it was because all holidays celebrated with friends and family always began and ended in the same place—the kitchen.

It is this love of cooking that made me decide to become a professional chef. Prior to becoming a chef, I was successful in the corporate world and even more successful as a stay-at-home mom raising my four children. It wasn't until my youngest son enrolled in kindergarten that I decided to change my love of cooking into a career. At the age of forty, I enrolled in culinary school and started on the path that has led me to where I am now: restaurant owner, chef and now cookbook author. I have two successful restaurants, Zapoteca Restaurante y Tequileria and Mixteca Taqueria, and get to do what I love every day . . . cook.

At the restaurants when I am walking the floor and visiting guests, I often get asked, "Why Mexican?" I guess it seems a bit odd for those who don't know me—that a blonde-haired, green-eyed woman is cooking traditional Mexican cuisine. To me, it's something that just seems natural.

During my youth in Oklahoma, I was surrounded by Mexican food and culture. Over time, I learned a deep appreciation for the Mexican people and their love of family, food and celebrations. As I continued my culinary education, I began researching and learning more about Mexican cuisine and the culture of the people that create it.

For a very long time, Mexican food has been underappreciated and underestimated around the world. It wasn't until recent years that the culinary community has really sat up and taken notice of the intricate flavors and techniques that Mexican food has to offer. Today Mexican food is finally being noticed and appreciated for all that it has to offer, not just its tacos and enchiladas.

In this book, I do include some recipes for tacos and enchiladas, but also more intricate and elegant recipes from around the Mexican country. I've made many of these recipes since I was a little girl, while others are based on my culinary training and research while traveling in Mexico. All recipes, however, represent food that I love and that satisfies my palate.

I love bold, memorable spices and unique flavor combinations. I love the surprise on the palate when you taste sweet flavors combined with a hint of spicy chile pepper. I love the brininess of not only seafood but also just the right amount of salt added to a dish to make it sing with flavor. I love the complexity of mole sauce that has been simmered for hours in such a way that the ingredients blend together as one to create the perfect marriage. I love the earthy taste of corn masa, whether it has been lightly grilled for tortillas or steamed in corn husks for tamales. These are the flavors that you will find in this book. At my restaurants, you can often hear me say that I want my guests to remember my food just as much as I want them to love it. I hope that you create memorable meals and flavors in your home using these recipes, flavors that you crave and want to cook and eat again and again.

Prior to each meal, my family gives a traditional toast stating what we are happy for. The toast always ends with the words *"a la familia"*—to the family.

So from my kitchen to yours, and from my family to yours, *"a la familia!"*

Shannon L. Bard

one

Fundamentos de México

INGREDIENTS, EQUIPMENT AND TECHNIQUES

If you've ever had the good fortune to visit a market in Mexico, you know that Mexico is virtually a cornucopia of ingredients. The Mexican open-air markets are overflowing with different kinds of chiles, nuts, seeds, fresh fish and produce as far as the eye can see.

These varieties of ingredients are what help make Mexican cuisine so unique. Luckily today as the palates of the world expand, so does the availability of international products here in the US. My jaw no longer drops to the floor when I see an entire aisle dedicated to Latin ingredients at my local grocery store. As a farmer's daughter, I also realize the importance of buying local products whenever possible and encourage you to do so when you can. The grocers are not the only ones increasing the number of Mexican products available; local farmers' markets throughout the country have expanded their crops to include produce such as tomatillos, jalapeños and squash blossoms.

In this section, I have listed ingredients that are mentioned throughout the cookbook that make a vital difference in the final flavor outcome of a dish. I've tried to list substitutions whenever possible, but at times, there simply are no suitable substitutions. I've also tried to only list the items that you may not be familiar with, and I have not created an enormous list of ingredients, as the vast array of Mexican ingredients is so large that entire books have been dedicated to them.

Many of the techniques listed are not dissimilar to those used in American kitchens. Roasting ingredients without oil (dry roasting) is an essential technique that imparts a slightly charred flavor and intensifies the taste of the vegetables. If you try only one technique in this book, that's the one that I suggest you try, as it could change the way you cook from now on.

The equipment necessary in Mexican cooking does not include elaborate, expensive tools. Cooking should be enjoyable, so if you do not have a tool listed, use what you have on hand to get the job done. If you don't have a molcajete, use a blender. After all, the molcajete is sometimes referred to as the "Mexican blender." The flavor outcome will be slightly different, but in the end, that is a small price to pay to keep your sanity and enjoy your time in the kitchen.

Anchiote Paste

Achiote paste, also called recado rojo, is a thick, deep red seasoning blend that is popular in the Yucatán region of Mexico. It is an essential ingredient in cochinita pibil but can also be used as a seasoning rub for pork, chicken or seafood. You can find achiote paste in Latin markets or in the Latin section of your gourmet grocery store. It is also very simple to make it yourself if you are feeling ambitious or can't find it anywhere.

Recado Rojo

ACHIOTE PASTE

YIELD: ½ CUP (115 G)

5 tbsp (50 g) annatto seeds

1 cup (240 ml) warm water

1 tsp cumin, ground

1 tsp dried oregano, preferably Mexican

5 cloves, whole

1 tbsp (8 g) black peppercorns

6 allspice berries

1 tbsp (15 g) salt

8 garlic cloves, peeled

1 habanero chile, seeded

¼ cup (60 ml) orange juice, preferably freshly squeezed

¼ cup (60 ml) white vinegar

2 lemons, juiced

2 tsp (10 ml) Herradura Silver tequila

Place the annatto seeds in the warm water and soak for 15 minutes to allow the seeds to soften slightly. Drain the seeds and place them in a coffee or spice grinder along with the cumin, oregano, cloves, peppercorns, allspice berries and salt. Grind the mixture to a fine powder.

Place the garlic, habanero, orange juice, white vinegar, lemon juice and ground spice mixture in a blender and blend for 2 minutes, or until you have a smooth paste. Add the tequila and blend on high speed for another 30 seconds.

Remove the mixture from the blender and refrigerate in an airtight container until ready to use.

Agave Nectar

Agave nectar, also referred to as agave syrup or aguamiel in Mexico, is used as a sweetener in a variety of sauces and drinks. It is slightly sweeter than honey and it's produced from several species of agave, including the blue agave, the plant from which tequila is made.

You can find agave nectar in the baking section of your local grocery store.

Canela

Canela, or Mexican cinnamon, has a flavor much more mellow and subtle than the typical cinnamon found in the US. It's also flakier and softer, which makes it much easier to grind for sauces.

Mexican cinnamon is used in a variety of sweet and savory dishes, and it's an essential ingredient in many moles. You can buy it at many Latin markets or order it online. If you can't find Mexican cinnamon, substitute 1 teaspoon of ground cinnamon for 1 Mexican cinnamon stick.

Cheese

QUESO CHIHUAHUA
Queso Chihuahua is a soft, white cheese that melts easily and is excellent in enchiladas or queso fundido. It is named after the Mexican state of Chihuahua, where it's from.

If you can't find queso Chihuahua, substitute Monterey Jack.

QUESO COTIJA
Queso cotija is a white, semi-firm, aged cheese that has a slightly salty flavor. Depending on the firmness, it is often grated or crumbled on top of dishes and salads.

Look for it in Latin markets or gourmet grocery stores. Substitute with Parmesan if necessary.

QUESO FRESCO
Queso fresco literally means "fresh cheese," and is a soft cheese with a mild, tangy flavor. It is most often found crumbled on top of soups and other dishes. It has become more common in the US and can be found in many Latin and gourmet grocery stores, or ordered online.

Feel free to substitute queso fresco for a mild feta cheese.

QUESO OAXACA
Queso Oaxaca is a type of cheese found in Mexico named after the southern state of Oaxaca, where it first originated. It has a close resemblance to mozzarella and is a great melting cheese, perfect for quesadillas.

If you can't find queso Oaxaca, substitute mozzarella.

Chiles, Dried

ANCHO

The ancho chile is the dried version of the poblano. It is about 4–5 inches (10–13 cm) long and has a deep reddish color, flat wrinkled skin and a heart shape. Its flavor is sweet with a fruity complexity.

The ancho chile can be used whole and stuffed to make a relleno, or rehydrated and ground to make moles and other sauces.

Because of its unique flavor, there are really no suitable substitutions for the ancho chile. You can find it in many Latin grocery stores or order it online.

CHILE DE ÁRBOL

The chile de árbol is a long, red, slender chile ranging in length from 2–3 inches (5–7.6 cm). It is related to the cayenne pepper and is very hot. The chile de árbol is readily available and great for sauces, salsas and soups.

Substitute cayenne pepper if you can't find chile de árbol.

CHIPOTLE

The chipotle chile is a smoke-dried jalapeño that has an intense heat and a complex, smoky flavor. Dried chipotles need to be rehydrated prior to use.

The most common way to find the chipotle chile today is canned and packed in an adobo sauce of tomatoes, vinegar, garlic and salt. Look for them in the Latin section of most grocery stores.

Any leftover chipotle chiles can be stored in an airtight container and refrigerated for up to 2 weeks.

GUAJILLO

Guajillo chiles are one of the most popular dried chiles in the US today and one of my absolute favorites. They are approximately 5–7 inches (13–18 cm) long with a shiny red skin. They have a sweet, unique, earthy flavor with a moderate heat level.

Guajillo chiles are most often pureed for salsas and moles.

They can be found at many Latin markets or ordered online.

MULATO

The mulato chile is a variety of the dried poblano and has a brown-black color with a wrinkled, prune-like skin. It has a mild taste with an almost chocolate-tobacco flavor.

The mulato chile is most often used in moles.

PASILLA

The pasilla chile, sometimes known as chile negro, is a dried chilaca chile. It is generally 6–8 inches (15–20 cm) long and narrow, with a shiny black skin. It has a rich, complex flavor with a slight hint of acidity and fairly hot heat intensity.

The pasilla is a very versatile pepper and can be stuffed or used in sauces and adobos.

Chiles, Fresh

HABANERO

Habanero chiles are small, extremely hot peppers that can range in color from green to orange to red. The oil from the habanero can be extremely painful if you get it in your eyes, so you should always wear gloves when handling them.

Today, habanero peppers can be easily found at most grocery stores. Substitute with serrano chiles if you are looking for a little less heat.

JALAPEÑO

The jalapeño is a medium-sized chile with varying levels of heat. Many think of the jalapeño as a hot pepper, but the heat can range from mild to very hot depending on how it is grown. If you are looking for more heat, be sure to leave the seeds in, as that is where the majority of the heat is.

Jalapeños are arguably the most common chile today; you can easily find them in Latin markets and your local grocery store.

POBLANO

Poblano chiles have a dark green exterior and an almost triangular shape and are relatively mild. They can be eaten raw but are often stuffed to make chile rellenos.

Poblanos can be found in the produce section of most grocery stores, but the Anaheim chile can be substituted if necessary.

SERRANO

The serrano chile is a thin, green pepper that is slightly smaller but much hotter than the jalapeño. It is great in salsas and guacamoles.

Serrano chiles are relatively easy to find at most grocery stores, but feel free to substitute jalapeños if desired.

Chorizo

Mexican chorizo is a fresh sausage made from ground fatty pork and seasonings. Don't confuse soft Mexican chorizo with dried, hard Spanish chorizo, as they are two completely different products. Most Mexican chorizo is red, although there are versions that are green and made with tomatillos.

Chorizo is a versatile ingredient and it's used in dishes like tacos, queso fundido and tortas. To cook it, the outside casing is removed and the ground meat is sautéed similarly to ground beef.

Mexican chorizo can be found in the refrigerated section of Latin or gourmet grocery stores or made at home.

Chorizo de Mexicana

MEXICAN FRESH SAUSAGE

YIELD: APPROXIMATELY 1½ POUNDS (675 G)

5 whole black peppercorns

3 whole cloves

¼ tsp ground cinnamon

½ tsp dried oregano, preferably Mexican

½ tsp dried thyme

2 tsp (5 g) paprika

2 tsp (10 g) salt

2 dried ancho chiles, stemmed, seeded, dry roasted and rehydrated (page 18)

1 dried guajillo chile, stemmed, seeded, dry roasted and rehydrated (page 18)

1 dried chipotle chile, stemmed, seeded, dry roasted and rehydrated (page 18)

1 chile de árbol, stemmed, seeded, dry roasted and rehydrated (page 18)

2 garlic cloves

3 tbsp (45 ml) apple cider vinegar

1 lb (450 g) fatty pork (I prefer pork shoulder), coarsely ground

Place the peppercorns, whole cloves, cinnamon, oregano, thyme, paprika and salt in a blender and blend until the peppercorns and cloves are completely crushed.

Add the rehydrated chiles to the blended spice mixture, along with the garlic and apple cider vinegar. Blend for 1 minute. If necessary, feel free to add up to ½ cup (120 ml) of water to the mixture to ensure that it is thoroughly blended.

Place the ground pork in a large, nonreactive bowl and top with the blended spice mixture. Using a large wooden spoon or your hands, thoroughly mix the pork and spices.

Cover the bowl tightly with plastic wrap and refrigerate for 12–24 hours to allow the flavors to combine. Freeze or refrigerate until use.

Note: The chorizo must be cooked thoroughly prior to being eaten.

Corn Husks

Corn husks are the papery, dried exterior of an ear of corn. They are used primarily for wrapping tamales. Prior to use, corn husks need to be soaked in warm water for 30 minutes to make them more pliable.

You can find corn husks at many well-stocked Latin markets or grocery stores, or purchase them online. Banana leaves can be substituted if necessary, but the flavor will be slightly different in the end product.

Mexican Crema

Mexican crema is the Mexican version of crème fraîche. Like crème fraîche, it is different than sour cream with a slightly tangier, softer flavor. Mexican crema is used in a variety of sauces and can also be used to top various dishes. You can find it at Latin markets and well-stocked gourmet stores, or better yet, make it yourself. Crème fraîche can be substituted if necessary.

Crema de Mexicana

MEXICAN CREMA

YIELD: 1 CUP (240 ML)

1 cup (240 ml) heavy cream, unpasteurized if available

3 tbsp (45 ml) buttermilk with active cultures

Place the heavy cream in a heavy-bottomed saucepan and cook over medium heat until the temperature reaches 95°F (35°C). If the temperature is too hot and exceeds 100°F (37.8°C), you run the risk of killing the active cultures in the buttermilk.

Remove the cream from the heat and slowly stir in the buttermilk. Place the mixture in a glass jar and top with the lid, leaving it slightly ajar. Place the mixture in a warm location and allow to rest undisturbed for 12–24 hours.

After the allotted time period, stir the mixture, tightly cover it and refrigerate for an additional 12–24 hours until it has thickened.

Herbs

EPAZOTE

Epazote is an herb originally native to Mexico but is now grown throughout the US. It is used to season a variety of dishes, including beans, soups, salads and even quesadillas. Epazote can be found both dried and fresh in many Latin markets and gourmet grocery stores. If available, the fresh option is always best.

Epazote has a distinct flavor that cannot be replaced with any other herb. If you do not have epazote, leave the herb out rather than trying to find a substitute.

MEXICAN OREGANO

Mexican oregano is an aromatic used in a variety of dishes throughout Mexico. There are countless varieties available in various regions of the country. Although it shares the basic pungent flavor of Mediterranean oregano, it has a slight citrus, licorice flavor.

Mexican oregano is available in Latin markets or it can be ordered online.

Masa

Masa is corn dough made from dried corn and lime. It is used in an array of items, including tortillas, quesadillas and sopes. If you are lucky enough to live near a tortilleria, you can buy it fresh. For those who don't have access to fresh masa, it can be made using masa harina and water. Masa harina comes in a bag similar to flour and is widely available in Latin markets and most grocery stores.

Nopales

Nopales are the pads of the prickly pear cactus. They can be eaten raw or cooked; however, the thorns need to be removed with a paring knife prior to cooking them. They have a light, salty flavor. When preparing, be careful not to overcook, as this will cause them to have a slimy texture.

Nopales are available in the produce section of many Latin markets and in some well-stocked grocery stores. When purchasing, look for fresh, firm nopales with a vibrant green color.

Pepitas

Pepitas, or pumpkin seeds, are the hulled green seeds from a variety of pumpkins. They add flavor and texture to many dishes and are often used as a thickener in moles.

Look for pepitas in Latin markets, health food stores and grocery stores.

Piloncillo

Piloncillo, also called panela, is made from pure, unrefined sugar that is pressed into a cone shape. Piloncillo is similar to brown sugar but with a much more pronounced molasses and sweet caramel taste. The cones are very hard and need to be cut with a serrated knife, or if necessary, broken into small pieces using a hammer.

You can find piloncillo at most Latin markets or substitute it for brown sugar.

Sea Salt

Salt is an essential ingredient in Mexican dishes. When I first began studying Mexican cooking, my instructor told me, "Mexican food is spicy; Mexican food is salty." Because of this, I prefer dishes with a little more salt, but not every palate is the same. In most recipes, I have listed salt to taste, and please do so.

I generally prefer to use sea salt because of its coarse, crunchy texture and strong flavor, but feel free to use table salt if that is what you have on hand.

Tomatillos

Tomatillos, also known as tomate verde, look like a green tomato covered with papery, dry husks. They have a bright acidic and tangy flavor. Tomatillos are used in a variety of sauces but are most well known for their use in salsa verde.

Prior to use, the outside papery husks must be discarded and the tomatillos rinsed thoroughly to remove the sticky coating.

Tomatillos are becoming more common in the US and can be found in Latin markets and the produce section of many grocery stores.

Essential Equipment

BLENDER
Although not a traditional piece of Mexican equipment, a blender will be one of the most helpful tools when preparing many of the dishes in this book. At the restaurant, we use blenders all day long to blend sauces and puree items for our moles.

When purchasing a blender, look for one with a larger cup so that you can puree sauces in fewer batches.

COMAL
The comal is an indispensable piece of equipment used in Mexican cooking. It is a smooth, flat griddle typically used to dry roast ingredients, toast spices and cook a variety of items, including the essential tortilla.

You can purchase a comal online, or invest in a cast-iron griddle available at your local kitchen shop.

MOLCAJETE

The molcajete is yet another indispensable item when preparing Mexican dishes. It is essentially a mortar made of volcanic rock that comes with a tejolote (pestle). It can be used to grind a variety of ingredients, but it's most often seen in Mexican restaurants in the US as a device to grind spices for tableside guacamole.

You can purchase a molcajete in Latin markets or order it online.

TORTILLA PRESS

When making tortillas, a sturdy tortilla press is extremely helpful. Large, square wooden presses and smaller, round metal presses are both readily available in the US. Both types work very well.

Traditional Techniques
Dry Roasting

Throughout this cookbook, a large number of recipes will call for ingredients to be roasted, or dry roasted. Dry roasting is a technique used in Mexican cooking that cooks ingredients in a dry skillet, without any oil or fat.

DRIED CHILES

Use a damp cloth to wipe the chile and remove any dust from its exterior. Using kitchen shears, cut off the stem and cut a slit along one side. Pry the chile open and remove the seeds. Depending on the recipe, you may need to keep the seeds to use in the final dish.

Heat a cast-iron pan or comal over medium-low heat until hot. Working in batches, open the chile and place it directly onto the pan, using tongs to push it down onto the pan. Cook the chile for 30-50 seconds, and then gently flip over and cook the other side for an additional 30-50 seconds.

Unless the recipe states otherwise, remove the toasted chiles from the heat and place in a large glass bowl and cover completely with warm water. If necessary weight the chiles down with a small plate to ensure that they are completely submerged. Soak the chiles for 30 minutes until they are completely softened. Drain the chiles and discard the soaking liquid.

FRESH CHILES

To dry roast fresh chiles (excluding poblanos), heat a cast-iron pan or comal over medium-high heat and place the chiles in the pan to cook, turning often, until they are blackened on all sides.

Some recipes call for the jalapeños to be peeled. If so, remove the jalapeño peppers from the heat and place in a glass bowl. Cover the bowl tightly with plastic wrap and allow the peppers to rest, covered, for 30 minutes, until the skin begins to separate from the flesh and the pepper is cool enough to handle. Remove the jalapeños from the bowl and use a paring knife to gently rub the skin off the pepper (in many instances, the skin will rub off using just your hand).

To seed the jalapeño, cut a slit from the tip to the base of the stem. Gently remove and discard the seeds and the ribs.

Habanero and serrano chiles do not need to be peeled.

GARLIC

Heat a cast-iron pan or comal over medium-high heat. Break the garlic cloves away from the head, place them in the pan and cook for approximately 4 minutes per side, until they're blackened in spots. Remove the garlic and let cool slightly before peeling.

ONIONS

Heat a cast iron-pan or comal over medium-high heat. Place a peeled and quartered onion in the pan and cook for approximately 15 minutes, turning occasionally, until the onion has softened and is blackened slightly.

POBLANO

Turn the flame on a gas burner to medium-high. Carefully place the poblano chile directly in the open flame and cook, turning often, until the pepper is completely blackened on all sides.

If you do not have a gas burner, position your oven rack approximately 8 inches (20 cm) under the broiler. Preheat the broiler to high and then place the poblano onto the rack and roast, turning often, until the poblano is blackened on all sides.

Repeat the same technique as described in the previous section with the jalapeño to peel and seed the poblano.

TOMATILLOS

Heat a cast-iron pan or comal over medium-high heat. Remove and discard the outside skin of the tomatillo. Gently rinse the tomatillo under cool water to remove the sticky outer coating, pat the tomatillo dry with a clean paper towel and place on the hot pan. Cook the tomatillo, turning once, until it is blackened on all sides but just before it is about to burst.

TOMATOES

Heat a cast-iron pan or comal over medium-high heat. Place the whole tomato directly onto the hot pan. Cook the tomato, turning once, until it is blackened on all sides.

If the recipe calls for the tomato to be peeled, place the tomato in a glass bowl and cover tightly with plastic wrap; let rest for 15 minutes until the skin has pulled away from the flesh and is cool enough to touch. Use a paring knife to gently peel away and discard the skin.

Making Tortillas

CORN

Freshly made corn tortillas, whether you are using fresh masa or reconstituted masa harina, have a much fresher, toasted flavor than the typical premade corn tortillas you purchase at your local market.

Making the perfect corn tortilla has many variables, but the most important one is practice. Don't worry if your initial tortillas aren't perfect; with a little practice, you'll never want to buy store-bought tortillas again.

Tortillas de Maiz

FRESH CORN TORTILLAS

YIELD: 24 TORTILLAS

---

2 cups (300 g) masa harina
½ tsp salt
1½ cups (360 ml) warm water

In a large mixing bowl, combine the masa harina and salt. Slowly pour the warm water into the corn mixture and mix with your hands until incorporated. Knead the mixture until you have one large ball of dough.

Pull a small bit of dough off of the larger piece and roll into a ball to test the consistency. Gently squish the ball between the palms of your hands until about ¼ inch (6 mm) thick. The dough should squish easily in your hands without being too sticky and form a flat disc with rounded edges. If the dough easily sticks to your hands, the mixture is too wet and you need to add more masa. If the dough forms a disc with rough edges when squished, the mixture is too dry and you need to add more water.

Pull an equal size portion of dough off of the larger piece and roll into a ball just larger than a golf ball. Place the masa ball onto a sheet tray lined with parchment paper and repeat the process with the remaining dough. You will need to cover the dough with a slightly damp towel as the masa can quickly dry out.

Heat a comal or cast-iron pan over medium-high heat.

Cut 2 (6-inch [15 cm]) round pieces of plastic from a shopping bag and place the first on the bottom of the tortilla press. Place the ball of masa onto the center of the plastic and top with the second piece of plastic. Close the cover of the tortilla press and apply enough pressure to flatten the dough into a 5-inch (13 cm) tortilla.

Lift the lid of the tortilla press and gently pull away the top layer of plastic. Flip the tortilla onto the palm of your hand and peel away the second piece of plastic.

Place the tortilla on the heated pan and cook for approximately 30 seconds, until the bottom starts to brown and bubble. Turn the tortilla over and cook the other side for an additional 30 seconds.

Remove the tortilla from the heat and set aside. Cover the cooked tortillas with a clean towel to keep warm. Repeat the process with the remaining dough, stacking the tortillas on top of one another after cooking. Serve immediately.

FLOUR

Like corn tortillas, fresh flour tortillas are extremely easy to make and have a unique flavor different than store-bought ones. In addition, homemade tortillas lack all of the binders and extra additives that you find in most store brands.

Tortillas de Harina

CLASSIC FLOUR TORTILLAS

YIELD: 24 TORTILLAS

3 cups (330 g) all-purpose flour, sifted

1 tsp baking powder

1 tsp salt

1 cup (240 ml) warm water

⅓ cup (80 ml) lard or vegetable oil, plus ¼ tsp for cooking the tortillas

Combine the flour and baking powder in the bowl of a stand mixer fitted with a dough hook. In another bowl, combine the salt and water until the salt is dissolved. Turn the mixer to medium speed and slowly drizzle the salt water mix and vegetable oil into the mixer bowl with the flour mixture. Continue to mix the ingredients for 1 minute, until the dough has formed into a ball. Feel free to add up to 2 tablespoons (30 ml) more water if the dough is too dry and not sticking together. Reduce the speed to low and continue to mix for 1 minute longer, until the dough is extremely smooth.

Remove the dough from the mixing bowl and place on a lightly floured surface. Divide the dough into 24 equal-size portions and roll each portion into a ball. Using the palm of your hand, flatten each ball to form a round disc. Place each disc on a lightly greased tray and cover with plastic wrap or a clean kitchen towel and set aside to rest at room temperature for 30 minutes.

Lightly oil a comal or cast-iron pan and heat to medium heat.

Place a dough disc on a lightly floured surface. Using a rolling pin, roll the disc into a 6-inch (15 cm) round tortilla. Place the tortilla on the heated pan and cook for approximately 1 minute, until it starts to brown and bubble. Turn the tortilla over and cook the other side for 30 seconds. Remove the tortilla from the heat and set aside to cool.

Repeat the process with the remaining discs, stacking the tortillas on top of one another after cooking.

Serve immediately.

two

Antojitos

STREET FOOD-INSPIRED STARTERS AND LIGHT MEALS

Over the last decade Mexican food has undergone a great transformation, and what was once seen as a cuisine consisting only of tacos and burritos now graces the tables of some of the world's best restaurants.

Although the food at these world-class restaurants is utterly amazing, the food from which it got its inspiration is worthy of a second glance as well. It's true that some of the tastiest food found in Mexico is served by the vendors along the streets and in the markets. From street tacos and tostadas to countless regional specialties, street food in Mexico is still some of the best food you will ever eat.

Overall, this chapter may seem a bit of a jumble of things you would serve as an appetizer, others that you would serve as a main course, but all are inspired by the street food of Mexico.

Jalapeños Rellenos de Queso

STUFFED JALAPEÑOS WITH CHIHUAHUA CHEESE

Jalapeño rellenos are very traditional in Mexico and so simple to make. Plump, spicy jalapeño peppers are stuffed with rich shredded cheese, dipped in a light egg-white batter and fried crisp until golden.

The creamy melted cheese helps soften the bold spice of the jalapeño peppers and the light egg batter adds a crisp textural contrast. Finish with a topping of chopped avocado and tomato to create a truly Mexican and flavorful dish.

These stuffed jalapeños are best eaten crisp right out of the fryer, or do as I do and fill your favorite taco with one.

YIELD: 12 RELLENOS

---

12 jalapeño chiles, dry roasted, peeled and seeded (page 18)

¾ cup (98 g) shredded Chihuahua or Monterey Jack cheese

2 cups (480 ml) canola oil, for frying

½ cup (60 g) all-purpose four

½ tsp salt

4 large eggs, separated (you'll only need the whites)

OPTIONAL, FOR GARNISH:

1 avocado, diced

Cilantro leaves, chopped

Mexican crema (page 15) or crème fraîche

Make a lengthwise slit from the base of the stem to the tip of each jalapeño. Gradually spoon 1 tablespoon (8 g) of cheese into each pepper and tightly squeeze it to close the sides around the shredded cheese. Place the prepared peppers on a wax paper–lined sheet tray and chill for a minimum of 1 hour, and up to 6 hours.

In a large sauté pan over medium-high heat, heat the canola oil to 350°F (177°C).

Meanwhile, add the flour to a shallow bowl and stir in the salt. Place the egg whites in a medium-size mixing bowl and using a whisk or mixer, gently beat the egg whites until soft peaks form.

Dredge the prepared pepper in the flour mixture and lightly shake to remove any excess. Hold the flour-dusted peppers by their stem and dip into the egg whites. Carefully lay the prepared peppers in the hot oil. Using a spatula or spoon, baste the peppers with the hot oil. Once the bottoms of the peppers are golden, turn them with a slotted spoon or spatula and brown the other side. Transfer to a wire rack or paper towel–lined plate to drain.

Garnish with diced avocado, cilantro and Mexican crema.

Note: Jalapeño peppers can range from mild to very hot. If you want to avoid the spicy flavor, look for jalapeño peppers that are larger without any markings along the sides. Jalapeños with tan colored flecks, or "tiger stripes," tend to be spicier.

Use Chihuahua cheese if you can find it; if not, Monterey Jack makes an excellent substitute.

Taquitos de Pollo

GOLDEN ROLLED CHICKEN TACOS

A taquito is a golden, rolled taco that's filled with shredded meat (and other fillings) and lightly fried. In this recipe, they are filled with moist chicken and fire-roasted poblano strips before being sprinkled with queso fresco and fresh avocado slices. Serve alongside spicy red chile salsa.

YIELD: 12 TAQUITOS

½ cup (20 g) fresh cilantro stems, chopped

2 tbsp (30 g) salt

1 tsp black peppercorns

2 garlic cloves

1 white onion, quartered

1 bay leaf

16 cups (3.8 L) water

4 boneless, skinless chicken breasts, rinsed

12 corn tortillas

2 tbsp (30 ml) canola oil

1 poblano chile, dry roasted, peeled, stemmed and seeded, cut into ¼" (6 mm)-wide strips (page 18)

½ cup (65 g) shredded Chihuahua or Monterey Jack cheese

2 cups (480 ml) vegetable oil

½ cup (65 g) queso fresco

2 tbsp (5 g) cilantro, chopped

2 avocados, pitted and sliced into ½" (13 mm)-thick strips

Spicy Red Chile Salsa (page 161)

Toothpicks or wooden skewers

Place the cilantro stems, salt, peppercorns, garlic, onion and bay leaf in a heavy 6-quart (6 L) stockpot and cover completely with the water; bring to a boil over medium-high heat. Add the chicken breasts to the boiling water. Simmer the chicken, uncovered, for 20 minutes, until cooked through and tender. Remove the pot from the heat and set aside to cool.

Strain the mixture through a colander and discard the garlic, onion and bay leaf. Roughly shred the chicken and set aside.

Preheat the oven to 350°F (177°C).

Spread the tortillas, overlapping as little as possible, across a large sheet pan. Lightly brush with the canola oil and cook for 1–2 minutes in the preheated oven until warm and soft.

Remove the tortillas from the oven and fill each with some chicken, a strip of poblano pepper and a spoonful of shredded cheese. Roll into a tight cigar and set aside, seam side down, on a platter. Place a toothpick or wooden skewer through the taquito to ensure that the seams stay tightly closed. Continue the process with the remaining tortillas.

Heat the vegetable oil in a heavy-bottomed sauté pan over medium-high heat until the oil is very hot. Place 2–3 taquitos in the pan at a time and fry for 4–6 minutes, turning once, until crisp and golden. Remove and place on a paper-lined plate to cool and drain. Repeat the process with the remaining taquitos.

Once cool enough to handle, remove the toothpicks from the taquitos, and arrange on a serving platter. Sprinkle with the queso fresco, chopped cilantro and top with avocado slices. Serve with a side of Spicy Red Chile Salsa.

Tacos al Pastor

SHEPHERD-STYLE PORK TACOS WITH PINEAPPLE HABANERO SALSA

The taco al pastor is the ultimate grilled taco. Pork loin is cut and marinated for hours in a spicy chile and orange mixture. Marinating the pork for such a long amount of time yields juicer, more evenly seasoned pieces of meat while the citrus helps tenderize the pork. The marinated pork is then grilled and complemented with charred, sweet pineapple salsa. The end result is an amazing taco that the entire family will love.

YIELD: 6-8 SERVINGS

½ cup (120 ml) orange juice, fresh

10 dried guajillo chiles, seeded, stemmed, dry roasted and rehydrated (page 18)

5 dried ancho chiles, seeded, stemmed, dry roasted and rehydrated (page 18)

5 dried pasilla chiles, seeded, stemmed, dry roasted and rehydrated (page 18)

Grated zest of 1 orange

2 tsp (8 g) light brown sugar

2 garlic cloves

1 tsp cumin seeds, toasted and ground

1 tsp toasted oregano, preferably Mexican

1 tsp salt

½ tsp black pepper

1 tsp white vinegar

1 tsp lime juice, fresh

3 oz (85 ml) cola

1 (3-4 lb [1.4-1.8 kg]) boneless pork loin, cut into ½" (13 mm) pieces

PINEAPPLE HABANERO SALSA

3 lb (1.4 kg) fresh pineapple, peeled, cored and cut into ¼" (6 mm)-thick rings

1 habanero chile, dry roasted, seeded and finely diced (page 18)

1 sweet red bell pepper, cored, seeded and finely diced

1 tbsp (2.5 g) cilantro leaves, finely chopped

1 tbsp (15 ml) lime juice, fresh

Salt

Fresh or good quality store-bought corn tortillas

1 lime, cut into wedges

In a small, heavy-bottomed saucepan, simmer the orange juice over medium-low heat for 5 minutes until slightly reduced. Remove from the heat and let cool slightly.

Add the reduced orange juice to a blender along with the rehydrated chiles, orange zest, brown sugar, garlic, cumin, oregano, salt, pepper, vinegar, lime juice and cola. Puree until extremely smooth. Pour the mixture into a baking dish, place the pork in the marinade and turn to ensure that each piece is thoroughly coated. Cover and chill for a minimum of 4 hours, and up to 1 day.

PINEAPPLE HABANERO SALSA

Heat an outdoor grill or grill pan to medium-high heat. Place the pineapple on the grill and cook until lightly charred on both sides. Remove the pineapple from the heat and dice into small ¼-inch (6 mm) pieces. Place the diced pineapple in a large bowl and gently stir in the habanero chile, bell pepper, cilantro and lime juice. Season to taste with salt.

Remove the pork slices from the marinade and place on the preheated grill. Cook for 2-3 minutes until slightly charred. Turn over and grill the other side for an additional 2 minutes. Transfer the pork to a cutting board and roughly chop.

Grill the tortillas for approximately 30 seconds per side, until warm and slightly charred.

Top each tortilla with a large spoonful of grilled pork, a tablespoon (10 g) of pineapple salsa and a squeeze of fresh lime.

Note: The original taco al pastor originated in the state of Pueblo and is Mexico's rendition of the Arabic shawarma, introduced by Lebanese immigrants in the 1960s. Today throughout the streets of Mexico you can see large iron rods stacked with meat roasting, ready to be made into delicious tacos. My version, luckily, does not call for stacking the meat on an iron rod and roasting for hours, but it is still essential that you marinate the pork for a minimum of 4 hours.

Tacos de Carne Asada y Hongos

MUSHROOM AND RED CHILE STEAK TACOS

One of my first experiences with Mexican street food was eating a carne asada taco served by a vendor in the streets of Tijuana, Mexico. The crispy, charred grilled meat combined with the rich chile sauce was a truly unique experience. In this version of carne asada tacos, flank steak is marinated in a flavorful, garlicky chile sauce, perfectly charred on the grill and topped with fragrant sautéed mushrooms. The earthy flavor is further intensified with a drizzle of black truffle oil and a dusting of chopped cilantro. Salsa Mexicana and guacamole make the perfect accompaniments to finish the ultimate street taco.

YIELD: 12 TACOS

RED CHILE-MARINATED STEAK
16 guajillo chiles, stemmed, seeded, dry roasted and rehydrated (page 18)

5 garlic cloves, dry roasted and peeled (page 18)

2 tsp (7 g) cumin seeds

½ tbsp (1 g) dried oregano

1 tbsp (15 ml) cider vinegar

3 cups (700 ml) vegetable or chicken stock

1 tsp canola oil

1 tbsp (12 g) sugar

1 tbsp (15 g) salt

2 lb (900 g) tri-tip or flank steak, trimmed of fat and silver skin and cut into ¼" (6 mm)-thick strips

Olive oil, to brush grill

GARLIC SAUTÉED MUSHROOMS
2 tbsp (29 g) unsalted butter

½ tbsp (7 ml) olive oil

¼ tsp dried oregano, preferably Mexican

¾ lb (340 g) good-quality mushrooms (I recommend a mixture of oyster, trumpet and shiitake), cut into ½" (13 mm)-thick slices

2 garlic cloves, finely chopped

1 tsp sherry vinegar

½ tsp salt

1 tsp black truffle oil

12 corn tortillas

OPTIONAL, FOR GARNISH
Salsa Mexicana (page 158)

Guacamole (page 169)

Queso fresco

Cilantro, chopped

Lime wedges

RED CHILE-MARINATED STEAK
In the cup of a blender or food processor, add the rehydrated chiles, garlic, cumin seeds, oregano, cider vinegar and 2 cups (475 ml) of the stock. Blend for 5 minutes until you have an extremely smooth puree.

Heat the canola oil in a heavy-bottomed saucepan over medium-high heat. Once the oil is hot and shimmering, add the chile puree all at once (be careful as it will splatter). Stir the mixture immediately and reduce the heat to medium-low. Simmer for 10 minutes, stirring often, until the sauce thickens and begins to darken.

Stir in the remaining 1 cup (225 ml) stock along with the sugar and salt. Continue to simmer for an additional 20 minutes to reduce.

Remove the sauce from the heat and season with additional salt, if desired. Transfer the sauce to a large, shallow baking dish and set aside to cool completely prior to marinating the steak. Place the steak strips in the chile marinade and turn to ensure that the pieces are thoroughly coated. Cover and refrigerate for a minimum of 1 hour (and up to 6 hours).

Preheat an outdoor grill or grill pan to medium-high heat. Brush the grill grates with olive oil to prevent the steak from sticking. Remove the steak from the marinade and place on the grill grates; cook for 2–3 minutes per side, turning once, until medium-rare. Remove the steak and transfer to a cutting board; allow to rest for 3–5 minutes before assembling the tacos.

GARLIC SAUTÉED MUSHROOMS
Heat the butter and olive oil in a large sauté pan over medium heat until hot and the oil mixture begins to shimmer. Add the oregano, mushrooms and chopped garlic and sauté for 3–5 minutes, stirring frequently to ensure that the mushrooms don't stick and the garlic doesn't burn. Stir in the vinegar, salt and truffle oil and cook for an additional 5 minutes, until the mushrooms are completely soft. Taste and season with additional salt if desired.

ASSEMBLING THE TACOS
To assemble the tacos, place a warm tortilla on a plate and add 3–4 pieces of steak. Top each taco with a spoonful of mushrooms, Salsa Mexicana and guacamole. Sprinkle with queso fresco, chopped cilantro and a squeeze of lime.

Note: If you are lucky enough to live in a region where wild mushrooms are abundant, please use whatever mushrooms are in season.

Huarache con Setas Silvestres

CRISP CORN MASA "SANDALS" WITH FRAGRANT MUSHROOMS

These corn masa "sandals" are very crispy and almost cracker-like. They're extremely light, yet sturdy enough to support a generous heaping of toppings. In this recipe, I've topped them with fragrant, garlicky mushrooms and fresh, crisp watercress. The earthy mushroom flavor is further intensified with a light drizzle of truffle oil. Feel free to omit the oil if it's not your thing, but I love the aromatic well-rounded flavor it adds to this dish. Topped with crisp watercress and a sprinkle of fiery Salsa Mexicana, the final dish makes a flavorful vegetarian starter or light meal.

YIELD: 4 SERVINGS

HUARACHE
1½ cups (227 g) dried masa harina

½ tsp salt

1 cup (240 ml) warm water

GARLIC SAUTÉED MUSHROOMS
2 tbsp (29 g) unsalted butter

½ tbsp (7 ml) olive oil

¼ tsp dried oregano

12 oz (340 g) assorted mushrooms, cut into ½" (13 mm)-thick slices

2 garlic cloves, finely chopped

1 tsp sherry vinegar

½ tsp salt

1 tsp black truffle oil

4 tbsp (60 ml) canola oil

OPTIONAL, FOR GARNISH
Salsa Mexicana (page 158)

Queso fresco or goat cheese, crumbled

Watercress leaves

Cilantro, chopped

HUARACHE
In a large mixing bowl, combine the masa harina, salt and water and mix thoroughly. Knead the dough for 2–3 minutes until smooth. Divide into 4 equal-size pieces and roll to form a cigar shape. Place the masa pieces between two pieces of lightly oiled parchment paper. Using a tortilla press or rolling pin, press each masa piece into a "sandal" shape, about ¼ inch (6 mm) thick. Loosely cover the pressed pieces with plastic wrap and set aside while you prepare the mushroom mixture.

GARLIC SAUTÉED MUSHROOMS
Heat the butter and olive oil in a large sauté pan over medium heat until very hot and the oil begins to shimmer. Add the oregano, mushrooms and garlic and sauté for 3–5 minutes, stirring frequently to ensure that the mushrooms don't stick to the pan and the garlic doesn't burn. Stir in the vinegar, salt and truffle oil and cook for an additional 5 minutes, until the mushrooms are completely soft. Taste and season with additional salt if desired. Set aside while you complete the masa harina sandals.

Heat 1 tablespoon (15 ml) of the canola oil in a large, heavy-bottomed sauté pan or cast-iron skillet over medium-high heat until the oil is hot and begins to shimmer. Gently place one huarache at a time in the skillet and cook for approximately 2 minutes until it begins to blacken on the bottom. Turn the huarache over and repeat with the other side for an additional 1–2 minutes. Transfer the cooked huarache to a serving plate and repeat with remaining 3 tablespoons (45 ml) of oil and 3 huaraches.

ASSEMBLING THE "SANDALS"
Spread ¼ cup (17 g) of the mushroom mixture on top of each huarache, and sprinkle with Salsa Mexicana and a handful of cheese. Top with watercress leaves and chopped cilantro.

Note: Never pick wild mushrooms yourself. Always ensure that your wild mushrooms are purchased from a reliable grocer or forager.

The huarache is a classic street snack from Mexico City that you can find throughout the country topped with a variety of items. The word *huarache* actually refers to both the street snack and the type of sandal. In fact, the snack huarache got its name because its shape resembles the flat sole of a sandal.

Huaraches con Chorizo, Papas y Aguacate

CRISP CORN MASA "SANDALS" WITH CHORIZO, POTATO AND AVOCADO

One of my absolute favorite combinations is spicy Mexican chorizo and potatoes. It's a traditional pairing found throughout Mexico that makes the perfect flavor marriage in a variety of foods, from taco fillings to side dishes.

In this recipe, I've topped a delicate, crisp corn masa huarache with this savory, spicy mixture of chorizo and potatoes. The crispness of the huarache creates a nice textural contrast to the soft potatoes, while the spicy, red chile chorizo adds just the right amount of heat. Finish with a topping of a few avocado slices and a sprinkle of chopped cilantro and queso fresco.

Better yet, leftover chorizo potatoes make a great taco filling and are excellent alongside your eggs for breakfast the next morning.

YIELD: 4 SERVINGS

HUARACHE

1½ cups (227 g) dried masa harina

½ tsp salt

1 cup (240 ml) warm water

4 tbsp (60 ml) canola oil

CHORIZO-POTATO MIXTURE

1 lb (450 g) red new potatoes, diced into ½" (1.3 cm) pieces

1 tbsp (15 ml) canola oil

12 oz (340 g) Mexican chorizo sausage

1 small white onion, finely diced

1 tsp salt

OPTIONAL, FOR GARNISH

1 ripe avocado, thinly sliced

Queso fresco

Chopped cilantro

Salsa Mexicana (page 158)

HUARACHE

In a large mixing bowl, combine the masa harina, salt and water and mix thoroughly. Knead the dough for 2–3 minutes until smooth. Divide into 4 equal-size pieces and roll to form a cigar shape. Place the masa pieces between two pieces of lightly oiled parchment paper. Using a tortilla press or rolling pin, press each masa piece into a "sandal" shape, about ¼ inch (6 mm) thick. Loosely cover the pressed pieces with plastic wrap.

Heat 1 tablespoon (15 ml) of the canola oil in a large, heavy-bottomed sauté pan or cast-iron skillet over medium-high heat until the oil is hot and begins to shimmer. Gently place one huarache at a time in the skillet and cook for approximately 2 minutes, until it begins to blacken on the bottom. Turn the huarache over and repeat with the other side for an additional 1–2 minutes. Transfer the cooked huarache to a serving plate and repeat with the remaining 3 tablespoons (45 ml) oil and 3 huaraches.

CHORIZO-POTATO MIXTURE

Bring a 6-quart (6 L) pot of water to a boil over medium-high heat. Add the diced potatoes and cook for approximately 10 minutes, until the potatoes are tender. Drain and set aside.

Heat the canola oil in a large sauté pan over medium-high heat until the oil begins to shimmer. Add the chorizo and cook for approximately 8 minutes, stirring often, until the fat renders and the chorizo begins to brown. Using a slotted spoon, remove the chorizo from the pan and place on a paper towel-lined plate to drain.

Add the potatoes and onions to the sauté pan containing the chorizo oil and cook for approximately 10 minutes, until the potatoes begin to brown and the diced onion is cooked through. Add the chorizo back to the pan and season to taste with salt.

ASSEMBLING THE "SANDALS"

Top each huarache with 1 cup (200 g) of the chorizo-potato mixture and 2 slices of avocado. Sprinkle each with crumbled queso fresco, chopped cilantro and plenty of salsa.

Note: You can make your own chorizo for this dish (page 14) or feel free to purchase good-quality Mexican chorizo at your local Latin market.

Empanadas de Pollo

ANCHO-GLAZED CHICKEN EMPANADAS

Once you take a bite of these flaky, crispy empanadas you won't be able to stop. They are that good. At the restaurants, I make a version with fresh rabbit, which is absolutely wonderful. Unfortunately, rabbit is not as readily available as chicken, so I have created this version, which is equally as amazing. Don't be frightened by the lengthy instructions; once you gather all of the ingredients, the process is much easier than it looks and well worth the effort. The ancho-dusted chicken tastes great on its own, but I love these empanadas served alongside Salsa Borracha for even more flavor impact.

YIELD: 24 EMPANADAS

ANCHO-DUSTED CHICKEN

3 lb (1.4 kg) whole chicken legs (including thighs), skin removed

1 tbsp (7 g) ancho chile powder

2 tbsp (29 g) unsalted butter

1 tbsp (15 ml) olive oil

2 cups (408 g) julienned white onion

1 garlic clove, dry roasted, and chopped (page 18)

1 cup (240 ml) dry white wine

3 cups (700 ml) chicken stock

6 Roma tomatoes, dry roasted and roughly chopped (page 18)

¼ cup (30 g) Mexican crema (page 15)

2 tbsp (30 ml) apple cider vinegar

2 tbsp (5 g) cilantro, chopped

1 tsp salt

¼ tsp freshly ground black pepper

EMPANADA DOUGH

4 cups (500 g) all-purpose flour

2 tsp (10 g) salt

1 tsp baking powder

⅓ cup (73 g) vegetable shortening or lard

4 tbsp (57 g) unsalted butter

1 large egg, slightly beaten

¾ cup (180 ml) warm water

2 cups (475 ml) vegetable oil, for frying

Salsa Borrracha (page 163, optional)

ANCHO-DUSTED CHICKEN

Generously rub the chicken legs with the dried ancho chile powder.

Heat the butter and oil in a large, heavy-bottomed pan or Dutch oven over medium-high heat until the oil is hot and begins to shimmer. Gently place the chile-rubbed chicken in the pan and cook for approximately 6 minutes, turning once, until the chicken is golden brown on all sides. Remove the seared chicken from the pan and place on a platter. Add the onions and garlic to the pan and sauté, stirring frequently, for 4–5 minutes, until the onions have softened. Add the white wine, stock and tomatoes to the pan and bring to a boil, stirring and scraping up any browned bits on the bottom. Return the chicken to the pan along with any of the accumulated juices on the platter. Immediately reduce the heat to medium-low and simmer the chicken for 15 minutes, covered. Turn the chicken over, cover and cook for an additional 10–15 minutes, until tender.

Remove the pan from the heat and transfer the chicken to a clean plate. Whisk the Mexican crema and vinegar into the remaining sauce and stir in the cilantro, salt and pepper.

When the chicken is cool enough to handle, pull the meat from the bones and roughly chop. Discard the bones and fold the chicken into the sauce. Taste and season with additional salt if desired. Set aside to cool completely before filling the empanadas.

EMPANADA DOUGH

Sift together the flour, salt and baking powder into a large bowl. Blend in the shortening and butter with your fingertips or a pastry cutter until the mixture resembles coarse sand. Whisk together the egg and water, and using a fork, gently stir into the flour-shortening mixture until thoroughly blended. Turn the dough out onto a lightly floured surface and knead for 1 minute until the mixture forms a solid, elastic ball. Loosely cover the dough with a damp cloth and set aside for 30 minutes.

Roll out the dough on a lightly floured surface until it is approximately ⅛ inch (3 mm) thick. Using a cookie cutter or rim of a large glass, cut the dough into large rounds. Cut the rounds as close to one another as possible as the dough cannot be rerolled. Discard any unused trimmings.

Lightly brush the edges of the dough with water. Spoon approximately 2 tablespoons (30 g) of the Ancho-Dusted Chicken filling onto the center of each round. Gently fold the dough over the filling and press the edges together to seal, and then crimp decoratively with your finger or a fork. Repeat the process with all the remaining empanadas.

Heat the vegetable oil in a heavy-bottomed sauté pan over medium-high heat until the oil is very hot. Place 2–3 empanadas in the pan at a time and fry for 4–6 minutes, turning once, until crisp and golden. Remove the cooked empanadas from the pan and place on a paper-lined plate to cool and drain. Repeat the process with the remaining empanadas.

Top with a drizzle of Salsa Borracha, or your favorite salsa.

Tamales de Chile Rojo Cerdo

RED CHILE PORK TAMALES

When I first tasted tamales I was a young girl and it was love at first bite. At their simplest, tamales are packets of corn dough stuffed with flavorful fillings and, in this case, wrapped in dried corn husks and steamed until plump. When masa is steamed it takes on a delicate, almost sweet, corn flavor. In this recipe, the tender masa is wrapped around a spicy red chile pork filling, which is absolutely amazing on its own but adds a nice, flavorful balance to the corn. If you've never made tamales before, don't be afraid. The process is quite simple once you get the hang of filling and wrapping the packets. You will have leftover pork from this recipe, so you might want to make a double batch of tamale batter, as they are incredibly delicious and go quickly. My family can't get enough of them and have been known to eat them cold right out of the refrigerator the next day.

YIELD: 24 TAMALES

RED CHILE PORK TAMALE FILLING

5 lb (2.3 kg) pork shoulder

1 tbsp (15 ml) canola oil, plus more for coating pork

4 tbsp (60 g) plus 1 tsp salt

2 tbsp (15 g) chipotle powder

14 dried guajillo chiles, seeded and stemmed

6 garlic cloves

1 tsp ground cumin

3 cups (700 ml) water

TAMALE DOUGH

3½ cups (596 g) masa harina

2¼ cups (532 ml) warm water

10 oz (284 g) lard or vegetable shortening

1½ tsp (6 g) baking powder

1½ cups (355 ml) chicken or vegetable broth

2 tsp (10 g) salt

32 dried corn husks

SPECIAL EQUIPMENT

Bamboo steamer or steamer tray for your stockpot

RED CHILE PORK TAMALE FILLING

Preheat the oven to 275°F (135°C).

Thoroughly rinse the pork shoulder with cool water and pat dry with a clean paper towel. Rub all sides of the pork shoulder with canola oil.

Combine 4 tablespoons (60 g) of the salt with the chipotle powder and rub the mixture on the pork, covering all surfaces. Set aside and let the pork rest at room temperature for 1 hour, but no longer. Resting longer than 1 hour will cause the salt to pull the moisture from the meat and make the pork tough.

After resting, place the pork in a deep roasting pan with the fat side down. Cover the pan with a tight-fitting lid or double layer of aluminum foil. Place the pan in the preheated oven and cook for approximately 3½–4 hours, until the pork falls apart when pressed with the back of a fork and reaches an internal temperature of 195°F (91°C). Remove from the oven and let rest (covered) for 30 minutes.

Using two forks, pull the pork into long strands. Resist the temptation to chop the pork into chunks. Strain the broth and reserve 4 cups (946 ml) of the pan drippings.

Meanwhile, heat a medium-size cast-iron skillet or heavy-bottomed sauté pan over medium-high heat. Once the pan is hot, cook the chiles for approximately 30 seconds per side, until they're slightly toasty. Be careful not to over-toast the chiles and allow them to turn black, as this will make the sauce bitter. Remove the toasted chiles from the pan and place in a bowl. Cover and completely submerge the chiles with hot water and set aside for 30 minutes to rehydrate.

After 30 minutes, remove the rehydrated chiles from the water with a slotted spoon and place in a blender. Discard the soaking liquid. Add the garlic, cumin, remaining 1 teaspoon salt and water to the blender. Puree until the mixture forms a smooth paste.

Heat the 1 tablespoon (15 ml) canola oil in a heavy, large stockpot over medium-high heat. When the oil is very hot and begins to shimmer, pour the red chile sauce into the pan and stir immediately. Be careful, as the sauce will splatter. Fry the sauce for 2–3 minutes, stirring constantly, until the sauce thickens and begins to darken. Add the reserved 4 cups (946 ml) of pork drippings and the pulled pork. Bring the mixture to a simmer and cook, uncovered, for 15 minutes. Set aside to cool slightly before preparing the tamales.

(continued)

Tamales de Chile Rojo Cerdo (continued)

TAMALE DOUGH

In a large bowl or the bowl of stand mixer, blend the masa harina with the warm water. Stir the mixture thoroughly to create a solid ball of rehydrated masa. Add the lard, baking powder, stock and salt, whisking thoroughly. If you are using a mixer, blend on medium speed for approximately 5 minutes. Set the mixture aside until ready to assemble the tamales.

ASSEMBLING THE TAMALES

Fill a large stockpot one-quarter of the way full with warm water and bring to a boil over medium-high heat. Roughly separate the corn husks and place in a large bowl or your sink and completely submerge in warm water. Allow the husks to soak for at least 30 minutes until they become relatively soft and pliable. Remove the husks from the water, separate completely and pat dry with a clean paper towel.

Prepare the ties for your tamales by tearing several of the husks into ½ inch (1.3 cm)-wide strips until you have 24 strips. Gently tie a knot at the narrow end of the strip and tear the opposite end to double the strip length to about 12 inches (30.5 cm) long. Continue this step for all of the strips and set aside.

Place a large corn husk on a clean flat surface with the shortest side facing you. Spoon approximately ¼ cup (60 g) of masa dough on the upper center of the husk and, using a butter knife or the back of the spoon, spread into a square shape across the width of the husk to approximately ¼ inch (6 mm) thick. Be sure to leave approximately ½ inch (13 mm) on the top and sides of the husks clean to allow for easier rolling.

Spoon approximately 2 tablespoons (30 g) of pork mixture in an even line along the center of the masa and gently fold the husk over widthwise to completely encase the filling and form a tight tube. Fold the bottom of the husk up toward the center of the tamale and tie with the prepared strip of corn husks. Be sure to leave the top of the husks open. Repeat the process with the remaining corn husks and masa dough.

Line a steamer basket with moistened corn husks. Place the prepared tamales upright with the open tops facing up in the steamer basket and top with additional corn husks. Cover the steamer basket with a tight-fitting lid and place on top of the stockpot with the boiling water and steam for 1 hour, until the batter separates easily from the husks.

Turn off the heat and allow the tamales to rest in the basket for 30 minutes until they begin to firm up before eating.

Note: When heating the water to cook the tamales, drop a clean coin into the boiling water. As the water boils, the coin will rattle, letting you know that the water has not boiled dry. If the coin stops rattling, you know that it is time to add more water.

Tamales were first developed as early as 5000 BC when a need for portable food was essential to the warring tribes in Mexico. Today, tamales are served throughout Mexico by street vendors from large, steaming pots.

Enchiladas Mineras

GUAJILLO CHILE AND CHEESE ENCHILADAS

The rich red chile sauce on this enchilada is one of my favorites. The guajillo chiles add an earthy, piquant flavor that balances out the slightly sharp taste of the fresh cheese. Traditionally, this enchilada contains grated raw onions and is topped with boiled, diced carrots and potatoes. My version uses the same ingredients but I've chosen to caramelize the onions to add an extra level of sweetness and lightly fry the carrots and potatoes to create a golden crisp finish to the dish.

YIELD: 12 ENCHILADAS

GUAJILLO CHILE SAUCE

16 guajillo chiles, stemmed, seeded, dry roasted and rehydrated (page 18)

2 garlic cloves, dry roasted (page 18)

3 Roma tomatoes, dry roasted (page 18)

½ white onion, dry roasted (page 18)

¼ tsp dried cumin

½ tsp dried oregano

2 tsp (10 g) salt

1 cup (240 ml) vegetable or chicken broth

1 tbsp (15 ml) canola oil

POTATO-CARROT GARNISH

¼ cup (60 ml) canola oil

1 Russet or Yukon Gold potato, cut into ⅛" (3 mm)-thick slices

1 large carrot, cut onto ⅛" (3 mm)-thick coins

⅛ tsp chile de árbol powder or cayenne pepper

Salt to taste

LIGHTLY CARAMELIZED ONIONS

1 tbsp (15 ml) canola oil

1 large white onion, sliced

¼ tsp salt

ENCHILADAS

12 corn tortillas, fresh or good-quality store-bought

2 tbsp (30 ml) canola oil

3 cups (390 g) queso fresco

1 cup (130 g) shredded Monterey Jack or Chihuahua cheese

GUAJILLO CHILE SAUCE

Preheat the oven to 350°F (177°C).

In a blender or food processor, combine the rehydrated chiles, garlic, tomatoes, onion, cumin, oregano, salt and broth. Blend for 2 minutes, or until you have a smooth puree. Add up to 1 additional cup (240 ml) of water or broth if necessary to reach the consistency of a thin tomato sauce.

Heat the canola oil in a heavy-bottomed saucepan over medium heat until shimmering, but not smoking. Pour the sauce into the pan all at once. Be careful as the sauce will splatter once it hits the oil. Stir the sauce immediately and cook for 5–7 minutes, or until the sauce begins to darken and thicken slightly.

POTATO-CARROT GARNISH

In a heavy-bottomed sauté pan, heat the canola oil until shimmering. Carefully place a handful of potato slices into the oil and cook for 2–3 minutes until they are golden brown. Make sure that there isn't too much crowding in the pan or the potatoes will be soggy. Remove the potatoes from the pan and place on a paper towel-lined plate to drain. Repeat the process with the remaining potatoes and carrots. Dust with chile de árbol and salt and set aside.

LIGHTLY CARAMELIZED ONIONS

Heat the canola oil in a wide, heavy-bottomed sauté pan over medium heat. Stir in the onion slices so that they are coated with oil. Sprinkle with the salt and cook for approximately 30 minutes, checking and stirring every 5 minutes to ensure that the heat is not too high and the onions are not burning. Once the onions are a light blonde color, remove from the heat and set aside.

ENCHILADAS

Spread the tortillas, overlapping as little as possible, across a large sheet pan. Brush the tortillas lightly with canola oil and place in the preheated oven for 1–2 minutes until just warm.

Spoon 1 cup (240 ml) of the guajillo chile sauce evenly onto the bottom of a heavy baking dish. Fill each tortilla with ¼ cup (32 g) of the queso fresco, 1 tablespoon (8 g) of the Monterey Jack or Chihuahua cheese and a small amount of caramelized onions. Roll each enchilada tightly and line in the baking dish, seam side down. Top the enchiladas with the remaining sauce. Bake, uncovered, in the preheated oven for 12–15 minutes, or until heated through and the cheese has melted. Remove from the oven and serve topped with crumbled queso fresco and the crisp potatoes and carrots.

Note: Enchiladas Mineras, or Miner's Enchiladas, are said to have originated in the Mexican state of Guanajuato when the wives of the mine workers prepared rich enchiladas for their working husbands.

Enchiladas Suizas

SWISS-STYLE ENCHILADAS

We serve a lot of enchiladas at both restaurants, literally hundreds a week, and this is by far the most popular. The rich, slightly citrus flavor of the sauce perfectly complements the delicate chicken to create an incredible light and easy meal.

The tomatillo cream sauce is extremely mild and comes together in a flash. Feel free to add more jalapeño to the sauce if you prefer a little more spice. You can also speed things up and omit poaching your own chicken and opt for a store-bought deboned, roasted chicken if you are running short on time. You are completely dependent, however, on a great melting cheese to make this dish memorable. Be sure to buy whole blocks and grate it yourself, rather than buying pre-shredded cheese as pre-shredded cheese often has chemicals added to keep it from sticking together in the bag and therefore doesn't melt as beautifully.

YIELD: 12 ENCHILADAS

POACHED CHICKEN
¼ cup (10 g) fresh cilantro, chopped

1 tbsp (15 g) salt

½ tsp black peppercorns

1 garlic clove

½ white onion, quartered

1 bay leaf

16 cups (3.8 L) water

4 chicken breasts, boneless, skinless and rinsed

SUIZAS SAUCE
10 tomatillos, peeled and dry roasted (page 18)

2 jalapeños, dry roasted and stemmed (page 18)

2 garlic cloves, dry roasted (page 18)

½ medium white onion, quartered and dry roasted (page 18)

1 bunch (14 g) cilantro, stemmed and coarsely chopped

2 tsp (10 g) salt

½ cup (60 g) Mexican crema (page 15)

ENCHILADAS
12 corn tortillas

2 tbsp (30 ml) canola oil

1 cup (130 g) shredded Chihuahua or Monterey Jack cheese

¼ cup (10 g) cilantro, chopped

½ small white onion, cut into rings

POACHED CHICKEN
Place the cilantro, salt, peppercorns, garlic, onion and bay leaf in a heavy 6-quart (6 L) stockpot, cover completely with the water and bring to a boil over medium-high heat. Cut and discard the excess fat from the chicken. Place the chicken breast in the boiling water and immediately reduce the heat to medium-low. Simmer the chicken, uncovered, for 20 minutes, until cooked through and tender. Remove the pot from the heat and set aside to cool. Once cool to the touch, remove the chicken from the stockpot and gently pull into long strands. Set aside.

SUIZAS SAUCE
Combine the tomatillos, jalapeños, garlic and onion in the bowl of a blender or food processor. Quickly pulse the ingredients 2–4 times until broken up and roughly chopped. Add the cilantro and salt to the chopped mixture and quickly pulse another 4–6 times until thoroughly blended and chopped. Pour the tomatillo salsa into a medium-size saucepan and heat over medium-low heat for 3–4 minutes until reheated. Remove from the heat and stir in the Mexican crema.

ASSEMBLING THE ENCHILADAS
Preheat the oven to 350°F (177°C).

Spread the tortillas, overlapping as little as possible, across a large sheet pan. Brush the tortillas lightly with canola oil and place in the preheated oven for 1–2 minutes until warm.

Evenly spread 1 cup (240 ml) of sauce onto the bottom of a heavy baking dish. Add a portion of the chicken to a tortilla and roll like a cigar. Repeat with the remaining tortillas and chicken. Top the rolled enchiladas with the remaining sauce and sprinkle with the cheese. Bake the enchiladas in the oven for 12–15 minutes, uncovered, until heated through and the cheese has melted. Remove from the oven and serve topped with fresh chopped cilantro and white onion.

Note : Enchiladas Suizas is a perfect example as to how Mexican food has evolved and been influenced by other cultures. Swiss immigrants brought dairy cattle with them to Mexico. This wider availability of creams and cheeses helped evolve this dish from being originally topped solely with salsa verde to now being topped with salsa verde combined with cream and cheese.

Enchiladas de Puerco

CHIPOTLE PORK ENCHILADAS WITH TOMATO HABANERO SAUCE

A version of this dish has been on the menu at both restaurants since we opened, and it continues to be one of our best sellers year after year. The rich pork pairs wonderfully with the subtle heat of the habanero sauce and the finish of raw red onion slices completes the nuance of flavors while also adding a nice crunch. If you love enchiladas, this dish is a must try. Serve with Clay Pot Beans (page 131) to create a full, memorable meal.

YIELD: 12 ENCHILADAS

CHIPOTLE PULLED PORK
2½–3 lb (1.1–1.4 kg) pork shoulder roast (Boston butt)

2 tbsp (30 g) salt

1 tbsp (9 g) chipotle chile powder

TOMATO HABANERO SAUCE
2 tbsp (30 ml) canola oil

½ medium white onion, sliced

8 Roma tomatoes, dry roasted and peeled (page 18)

1 cup (240 ml) chicken broth

1 habanero chile, cut in half

1 tsp salt

ENCHILADAS
12 corn tortillas, fresh or good-quality store-bought

2 tbsp (30 ml) canola oil

1 cup (130 g) shredded Monterey Jack or Chihuahua cheese

½ red onion, thinly sliced

CHIPOTLE PULLED PORK
Preheat the oven to 275°F (135°C).

Rinse the pork roast under cool water and lightly pat with a paper towel to dry. Combine the salt and chipotle powder in a small bowl and thoroughly rub the mixture onto the pork, being sure to completely cover all surfaces. Place the pork in a roasting pan or Dutch oven and cover tightly with a lid or double layer of aluminum foil. Place in the preheated oven and cook for 3½–4 hours, until the pork is extremely tender and falls apart when pressed with a fork or tongs.

Remove the cooked pork from the oven and let rest, covered, for 15 minutes. Remove from the pan and using two forks, shred into large strands. Discard the pan drippings and set the shredded pork aside.

TOMATO HABANERO SAUCE
Heat 1 tablespoon (15 ml) of the canola oil in a medium sauté pan over medium-high heat until it shimmers. Place the sliced onions in the pan and cook, stirring often, for 7–10 minutes, until the onions are extremely soft but not yet browning. Then, using a slotted spoon, remove the onions from the sauté pan and place in a blender along with the tomatoes; blend for 2 minutes until the mixture is smooth and a warm orange color.

Heat the remaining 1 tablespoon (15 ml) canola oil in a heavy-bottomed saucepan over medium heat and pour the sauce into the pan all at once. Be careful, as the sauce will splatter. Stir and cook for 3 minutes, or until it begins to darken and thicken slightly. Add the broth, habanero pepper and season with salt. Reduce the heat to medium-low and simmer the sauce for an additional 3–5 minutes, until thoroughly heated. Taste the sauce. If the habanero has added enough heat for your palate, remove it with a slotted spoon. If you prefer more heat, continue to cook the sauce with the pepper until you've reached your desired heat level. Remove the pepper before serving.

ASSEMBLING THE ENCHILADAS
Preheat the oven to 350°F (177°C).

Spread the tortillas, overlapping as little as possible, across a large sheet pan. Brush the tortillas lightly with canola oil and place in the oven to heat for 1–2 minutes, until just warm.

Spoon 1 cup (240 ml) of the Tomato Habanero Sauce evenly onto the bottom of a heavy baking dish. Fill each tortilla with ¼ cup (50 g) of shredded pork and 1 tablespoon (8 g) of shredded Monterey Jack or Chihuahua cheese. Roll each enchilada tightly and place in the baking dish, seam side down. Top the rolled enchiladas with the remaining sauce and an additional sprinkling of shredded cheese. Bake in the preheated oven, uncovered, for 12–15 minutes, or until heated through and the cheese has melted. Remove from the oven and serve topped with thinly sliced red onions.

Note: The leftover pulled pork can be used for a fantastic taco filling or to make Red Chile Pork Tamales (page 41).

Quesadillas de Flor de Calabaza

SQUASH BLOSSOM QUESADILLAS

You might never have thought of eating the squash blossoms from your garden, but in the summer when they are in full bloom, this quesadilla makes an excellent and visually stunning starter or light meal. The subtle flavor of zucchini or yellow squash provided by the blossoms pairs wonderfully well with the slight heat of the poblano chile. The melted cheese brings the familiarity back to the quesadilla with its rich creaminess. Top with Roasted Tomatillo Salsa to add another layer of spice.

YIELD: 12 QUESADILLAS

12 oz (341 g) squash blossoms

1 tbsp (15 ml) canola oil

¼ cup (38 g) diced white onion

2 garlic cloves, minced

2 poblano chiles, dry roasted, stemmed, seeded and roughly chopped (page 18)

1 cup (130 g) shredded Oaxaca or mozzarella cheese

2 tsp (2 g) cilantro leaves, chopped

½ tsp salt

12 corn tortillas, fresh or good-quality store-bought

Roasted Tomatillo Salsa (page 157), or your favorite store-bought salsa

Remove the stems from the green base of the squash blossoms and lightly pluck out the pistil from inside the flower. Discard both the stems and the pistils. Rinse the blossoms under lightly running, cool water and place on a paper towel to dry. Once the blossoms have dried, roughly chop them.

Heat the canola oil in a heavy-bottomed sauté pan over medium heat until hot, but not smoking. Stir in the diced onion and cook for 2-3 minutes. Add the minced garlic, poblano chiles and squash blossoms to the pan and cook, stirring often, for about 5 minutes, or until the onions are translucent and the green bases of the blossoms have softened.

Remove the pan from heat and let cool for 10 minutes. Stir in the shredded cheese and chopped cilantro. Season with salt.

Heat a large cast-iron skillet or comal over medium heat. Once hot, place a tortilla directly onto the bottom of the pan. Immediately spoon 3-4 tablespoons (30-40 g) of the filling onto the center of the tortilla and spread so that it covers half of the tortilla. Gently fold the tortilla in half over the filling and continue cooking for another 1-2 minutes, until the bottom of the tortilla is golden brown. Flip the tortilla over and cook the other side for another 1-2 minutes in the same way. Remove from the heat and set aside on a plate to cool slightly. Repeat the process with the remaining tortillas. Serve with the Roasted Tomatillo Salsa or your favorite store-bought salsa.

Note: Squash blossoms are available at farmers' markets from May to August, depending on where you live. They are commonly used for flavoring in a wide variety of Mexican dishes and are considered a true delicacy.

three

Carne y Aves

MEAT AND POULTRY

At the restaurants, I am known for my intricate sauces full of depth and flavor. From the rich, dark moles to the slightly spicy ancho sauce topping for our Filete con Champinones, all are delicious. There are literally hundreds of different versions of mole, but the one most well known (and my favorite) is the Mole Poblano, with its rich depth of flavor and just a hint of chocolate.

This chapter contains my version of Mole Poblano, inspired by my first instructor, Chef Iliana de la Vega, along with other traditional and not so traditional moles. If you've never made mole, you definitely should. It's not nearly as difficult as the long list of ingredients leads you to believe and the end result is worth every single second in the kitchen.

All of the recipes in this chapter are full of rich, bold flavors that I love so much. They are all equally memorable and beautiful enough to be a showstopper at your next family dinner or party.

Pollo Encacahuatado

CHICKEN IN PEANUT SAUCE

Whenever I teach a Mexican cooking class that contains Pollo Encacahuatado, it is always the class's favorite. The nutty flavors are extremely complex for a sauce that takes so little time to make. The rich flavor of the peanut sauce is spiced with chipotle chiles, cloves and cinnamon. The sauce is then simmered slowly before adding the chicken pieces, which are lightly fried rather than sautéed, which is the traditional method in Mexico. Lightly frying the chicken helps retain moisture and adds an extra dimension of flavor.

YIELD: 6 SERVINGS

CHICKEN
1 cup (240 ml) peanut oil

1 tbsp (15 g) salt

¼ tsp ground chile de arbol or cayenne pepper

½ cup (63 g) all-purpose flour

1 (3–4 lb [1.4–1.8 kg]) whole chicken, skinned, back bone removed and cut into 8 pieces

PEANUT SAUCE
2 cups (322 g) raw peanuts

½ tsp whole peppercorns

¼ tsp whole cloves

4 Roma tomatoes, dry roasted (page 18)

½ white onion, dry roasted and peeled (page 18)

4 garlic cloves, dry roasted and peeled (page 18)

2 tsp (5 g) cinnamon

3 chipotle chiles en adobo

4 cups (1 L) chicken broth

2 tbsp (30 ml) peanut oil

Preheat the oven to 350°F (177°C).

CHICKEN
Heat the peanut oil in a large Dutch oven over medium-high heat.

In a shallow pan or baking dish, stir the salt and chile de árbol powder into the flour. Gently dredge the chicken pieces in the flour and lightly shake to remove any excess.

When the oil is hot (but not smoking), fry the chicken, working in batches, for approximately 5 minutes, until the bottom is lightly browned. Use tongs to turn the chicken pieces over and cook for an additional 5 minutes. Remove from the oil and place on a paper towel-lined tray to drain. Repeat the process with the remaining chicken pieces.

PEANUT SAUCE
Place the peanuts on a shallow baking sheet in an even layer. Bake in the preheated oven for 10 minutes, stirring once, until the peanuts are lightly toasted. Set aside to cool.

Heat a small sauté or cast-iron pan over medium-high heat. Once hot, place the peppercorns and whole cloves in the pan and lightly toast for 2 minutes until fragrant.

Place the peanuts, tomatoes, onion, garlic, cinnamon, peppercorns, cloves, chiles and 1 cup (240 ml) of the chicken broth in a blender. Blend for 3 minutes until the mixture is extremely smooth.

Heat the peanut oil in a large Dutch oven over medium-high heat. When the oil is very hot and begins to shimmer, add the blended mixture all at once into the pan and immediately stir. Be careful, as the sauce will splatter. Fry for 2–3 minutes, stirring constantly, until the sauce thickens and begins to darken.

Stir the remaining 3 cups (700 ml) chicken stock into the sauce and add the chicken pieces. Gently spoon the sauce over each piece to ensure that it's evenly coated. Cover the pan and cook for an additional 30 minutes, until the chicken is tender and falling off the bone. Remove from the heat and enjoy.

Note: It's also great over rice.

Pollo en Mole Poblano

SPICE-RUBBED ROASTED CHICKEN WITH PUEBLO-STYLE MOLE

There isn't a more beloved mole in Mexico than Mole Poblano, and with its rich, deep, complex flavor it is easy to see why. This version is inspired by the Mole Poblano that was taught to me by Chef Iliana de la Vega of El Naranjo restaurant in Austin, Texas.

In Mexico, you will find shredded chicken doused with rich Mole Poblano. My version takes the decadence to a new level by combining rich Mole Poblano with crispy roasted chicken spiced with coriander and black peppercorns.

YIELD: 6 SERVINGS

MOLE POBLANO
¼ cup (60 ml) lard or canola oil, plus more as needed

4 mulato chiles, stemmed and seeded (seeds reserved)

3 ancho chiles, stemmed and seeded (seeds reserved)

3 pasilla chiles, stemmed and seeded (seeds reserved)

3 tomatillos, quartered

2 Roma tomatoes, quartered

1 tsp black raisins

10 whole almonds

1 oz (28 g) pumpkin seeds

5 black peppercorns

1 whole clove

½ tsp ground cinnamon or Mexican canela

¼ tsp coriander seeds

¼ tsp anise seeds

¼ tsp ground allspice

⅛ tsp dried marjoram

¼ cup (40 g) sesame seeds

2 stale tortillas, lightly toasted

½ white onion, dry roasted and peeled (page 18)

2 garlic cloves, dry roasted and peeled (page 18)

5 cups (1200 ml) vegetable or chicken broth

2-4 tbsp (24-48 g) sugar

2 oz (57 g) Mexican chocolate

1 tsp salt

SPICE-RUBBED CHICKEN
1 (3-4 lbs [1.4-1.8 kg]) whole chicken

1 tsp coriander seeds

½ tsp black peppercorns

1½ tsp (7.5 g) salt

1 tbsp (15 ml) olive oil

1 tbsp (14 g) unsalted butter

GARNISH
2 radishes, thinly sliced

2 tbsp (20 g) sesame seeds, lightly toasted

MOLE POBLANO

Heat 1 tablespoon (15 ml) of the oil or lard in a large sauté pan over medium heat until shimmering. Add the mulato chiles and cook for approximately 1 minute on both sides until the skin begins to darken slightly. Remove the chiles from the heat and place in a bowl filled with warm water to rehydrate. Repeat the process with the remaining ancho and pasilla chiles, watching closely as some types of chiles cook faster than others. Soak all the chiles together for 15 minutes to soften.

Return the pan to the heat, adding more oil if necessary to ensure that the bottom of the pan is evenly coated. Cook the tomatillos and tomatoes for approximately 3-4 minutes, until the tomatoes begin to soften. Using a slotted spoon, remove the tomatillos and tomatoes from the pan and place in an extra-large bowl.

Return the pan to the heat, adding more oil if necessary to ensure that the bottom of the pan is evenly coated. Sauté the raisins, almonds and pumpkin seeds for 2 minutes, until the raisins are plump and the pumpkin seeds begin to turn a light, golden brown. Place in the bowl along with the tomatillos and tomatoes. Combine the reserved chile seeds, peppercorns, clove, cinnamon, coriander, anise, allspice, marjoram and sesame seeds and sauté for 2-3 minutes, stirring frequently, until the sesame seeds are lightly toasted and the spices have released their aroma. Place in the extra-large bowl with the other ingredients. Add the tortillas, onion and garlic to the mixture. Add the mixture to a blender, in batches if necessary, along with 2 cups (474 ml) of the chicken or vegetable broth and puree until extremely smooth. Strain through a small-mesh strainer and set aside.

(continued)

Pollo en Mole Poblano (continued)

Drain the chiles and discard the soaking liquid. Place the chiles in a blender along with 2 cups (480 ml) of the vegetable or chicken broth and puree until very smooth. Pass through a fine-mesh strainer, discarding the large particles, and set aside.

Heat the remaining 3 tablespoons (45 ml) oil in a heavy stockpot over medium-high heat. When the oil is very hot and begins to shimmer, pour the pureed chile mixture into the pan and immediately stir. Be careful, as the sauce will splatter.

Cook the puree for 15 minutes, stirring frequently, until it changes color and begins to darken. Reduce the heat to medium and stir in the pureed vegetable-spice mixture and cook for an additional 30 minutes to blend all the flavors. Thin the mixture slightly with the remaining 1 cup (240 ml) chicken broth and stir in 2 tablespoons (24 g) of the sugar, 1 ounce (28.5 g) of the chocolate and the salt. Continue to cook the mixture, stirring often, for another 30 minutes. Taste and season with additional salt, and the remaining 1 ounce (28.5 g) chocolate, and the remaining 2 tablespoons (24 g) sugar if desired.

SPICE-RUBBED CHICKEN
Preheat the oven to 400°F (204°C).

Using kitchen shears or a very sharp knife, cut the chicken along both sides of the backbone to remove it. Place the chicken, skin side up, on a cutting board and use the palm of your hands to firmly press down on the bird to flatten. Rinse thoroughly under cool running water and pat dry with clean paper towels.

Place the coriander seeds and peppercorns in a spice grinder and grind until smooth. Mix with the salt and thoroughly rub on all sides of the chicken.

Heat the olive oil and butter in a cast-iron or heavy-bottomed sauté pan over medium-high heat until very hot, but not smoking. Place the chicken in the pan, skin side down, and cook for 4–5 minutes, until the skin has turned a golden brown and begun to crisp.

Using tongs, gently turn the bird over and place in the preheated oven to cook for approximately 45 minutes, or until the internal temperature has reached 165°F (74°C).

Remove the cooked chicken from the oven and let rest for 5 minutes prior to cutting. Cut into 8 pieces and place on plates or a serving platter. Top with the Mole Poblano sauce and garnish with the radish slices and a sprinkle of sesame seeds.

Note: Because the flavors are so complex, this dish pairs surprisingly well with the full-bodied flavors of Herradura Anejo tequila or a rich Spanish red wine such as Priorat.

Pato con Mole Arándano

ADOBO-GLAZED DUCK BREAST WITH CRANBERRY-PECAN MOLE

The lush mole in this dish is extremely elegant and with the addition of pecans and tart cranberries, slightly different than the traditional moles of Mexico. The cinnamon and cloves in the mole even further enhance the spicy sweetness of the overall dish.

Duck breasts are first scored and coated in a rich, traditional adobo sauce of garlic and fruity ancho chile peppers and then pan-seared and crisped before being topped with this sultry mole sauce.

Pair with the Cranberry Sage Margarita (page 185) to further accentuate the cranberry flavor and create a truly elegant meal for entertaining.

YIELD: 6 SERVINGS

CRANBERRY NUT MOLE
6 guajillo chiles, stemmed, seeded, dry roasted and rehydrated (page 18)

12 ancho chiles, stemmed, seeded, dry roasted and rehydrated (page 18)

½ cup (80 g) sesame seeds

1–2 cups (240–480 ml) water

4 tomatillos, dry roasted (page 18)

4 tbsp (60 ml) canola oil

5 oz (142 g) pecans

5 oz (142 g) dried cranberries, plus more for garnish

6 garlic cloves, dry roasted and peeled (page 18)

¾ tsp ground cinnamon or Mexican canela

1 tsp salt

¼ tsp pepper

6 whole coves

1 tortilla

1 oz (28 g) Mexican chocolate

4 cups (960 ml) chicken or vegetable stock

Salt

4–5 tbsp (48–60 g) sugar

ADOBO
6 dried ancho chile peppers, stemmed, seeded, dry roasted and rehydrated (page 18)

2 garlic cloves

1 tsp oregano, preferably Mexican

1 tsp salt

½ tsp black pepper

⅛ tsp ground cloves

4 tsp (16 g) sugar

⅓ cup (79 ml) apple cider vinegar

DUCK
6 (5–6-oz [142–170 g]) boneless duck breasts, halved, skin and fat trimmed

Salt

2 tbsp (30 ml) canola oil

CRANBERRY NUT MOLE
Place the rehydrated guajillo and ancho chiles in a blender along with the water and thoroughly blend. Feel free to add some or all of the remaining 1 cup (240 ml) water, if necessary, to form a very smooth puree. Strain through a fine-mesh strainer and discard any large particles. Set aside.

Heat a large cast-iron pan or comal over medium-high heat. Once the pan is very hot, add the sesame seeds and toast for 1–2 minutes, until just golden brown. Remove the sesame seeds and place in a blender along with the roasted tomatillos. Return the pan to the heat and add 2 tablespoons (30 ml) of the canola oil. Once the oil is very hot, place the pecans in the pan and cook, stirring often, for approximately 3 minutes, until the pecans begin to darken slightly. Remove the pecans from the pan with a slotted spoon and add to the blender with the tomatillos and sesame seeds. Repeat the same process with the dried cranberries.

Add the garlic, cinnamon, salt, pepper, cloves, tortilla, chocolate and 3 cups (720 ml) of the chicken broth to the blender and blend to a smooth puree. Strain the mixture through a fine-mesh strainer and discard any large particles.

(continued)

Pato con Mole Arándano (continued)

Heat the remaining 2 tablespoons (30 ml) canola oil in a stockpot over medium heat. Once the oil is hot, add the pureed chile mixture, stir and cook for 10 minutes until it changes color and begins to thicken.

After 10 minutes, add the tomatillo-puree mixture and stir to blend; cook for another 5 minutes. Stir in the remaining 1 cup (240 ml) broth. Simmer over low heat for 30 to 40 minutes, stirring often.

Season with salt. Add the sugar 1 tablespoon (12 g) at a time, tasting to ensure that the mole does not become too sweet. Keep the mixture warm while your prepare the remaining items.

ADOBO
Combine the chiles, garlic, oregano, salt, pepper, cloves, sugar and vinegar in a blender. Blend to a smooth puree and set aside.

DUCK
Preheat the oven to 400°F (204°C).

Gently score the skin of the duck, being careful not to cut into the flesh, with 4 diagonal cuts in one direction followed by 4 diagonal cuts in the opposite direction, forming a diamond pattern. Liberally rub the duck breast with the adobo and sprinkle with salt.

Place an extra-large cast-iron or ovenproof sauté pan over medium-low heat until very hot. Pour 2 tablespoons (30 ml) of the canola oil into the pan and heat until shimmering. Place the duck, skin side down, in the heated pan. Cook for approximately 5 minutes, or until the skin is crisp and golden brown. Gently turn the duck over and cook the opposite side for 1 minute. Place the pan in the oven and cook for an additional 8 minutes, or until the internal temperature has reached 125°F (52°C) for medium-rare.

Transfer the duck breasts to a cutting board and let rest for 5 minutes. Carefully slice each breast on a slight diagonal and place on a platter or serving tray. Spoon mole on top of the duck and garnish with additional dried cranberries if desired.

Note: Game birds, such as duck, have been part of the Mexican diet since pre-Hispanic times. Duck is now used throughout Mexico in everything from tacos to carnitas.

Carnitas de Puerco

MEXICAN PULLED PORK WITH CITRUS AND CUMIN

Carnitas are prepared in different ways throughout Mexico depending on where you eat them, but this is my family's absolute favorite.

Bits of pork are spiced with orange and cumin and simmered for hours until they become super juicy, yet delectably crispy. The addition of the sweetened condensed milk adds a hint of sweetness and helps with the browning process. The final dish is incredibly simple to make and completely wonderful. Paired with rice, the juicy pork makes an excellent meal by itself or as a filling for tacos and tamales.

YIELD: 6-8 SERVINGS

1 (5-6 lb [142-170 g]) pork shoulder roast (Boston butt)

2 tsp (5 g) ground cumin

2 tsp (1 g) dried oregano, preferably Mexican

3 garlic cloves, peeled and crushed

2 oranges, halved

1 lime, halved

2 bay leaves

1 white onion, peeled and quartered

2 tbsp (30 ml) sweetened condensed milk

1 (12 oz [340 ml]) can Mexican beer

4 cups (960 ml) cold water

2 tsp (10 g) salt

OPTIONAL, FOR SERVING
Warm tortillas

Fresh Avocado Guacomole (page 169)

Salsa Mexicana (page 158)

Rinse the pork shoulder under cool running water and pat dry with a clean paper towel. Move to a cutting board and cut into 2-inch (5 cm) pieces. Try to cut the pieces as uniform as possible, as this will ensure that the carnitas cook evenly. Don't worry about trimming the fat as it will render during the cooking process and it is necessary to crisp the pork during the final stages of cooking.

Place the pork pieces in a large, heavy-bottomed stockpot or Dutch oven and toss with the cumin and oregano. Add the garlic, 2 of the orange halves, lime halves, bay leaves, onion and sweetened condensed milk to the pan and pour the beer on top.

Cover the entire mixture with the water and bring to a boil, uncovered, over medium-high heat. Once the mixture reaches a boil, reduce to medium and continue simmering, stirring occasionally, for 1½-2 hours, until the pork is fork-tender and all of the liquid has evaporated. You will need to stir more often as the liquid evaporates to ensure that the pork does not stick to the bottom of the pan.

Preheat the oven to 425°F (218°C).

Once all of the liquid has evaporated, transfer the pork to an ovenproof dish (if not using a Dutch oven) and discard the bay leaves, onion, orange and lime. Sprinkle with the salt and pour any remaining pan drippings into the roasting dish. Cook, uncovered, for 15 minutes, until golden brown.

Remove the pork from the oven and squeeze the juice of the remaining 2 orange halves on top. Serve with warm tortillas, guacamole and salsa, if desired.

Note: Carnitas literally means "little meats."

Costillas Adobadas

MEZCAL-BRAISED SPARE RIBS WITH SPICY CHIPOTLE MOLASSES SAUCE

When I first began developing this recipe, I searched for a way to get a great smoky flavor without having to use an outdoor smoker or processed smoke-flavored seasonings. What better way to impart a smoke flavor than to steam the seasoned ribs in smoky mezcal? This process takes a while but it involves surprisingly little work. Costillas Adobadas is a great make-ahead dish for a backyard grill party, as you only need to reheat and glaze the finished product. The final drizzle of the Chipotle-Molasses Sauce gives just the right kick and forms a sweet and sticky glaze that adds a touch of moisture to the charred ribs.

YIELD: 4-6 SERVINGS

MEZCAL-BRAISED RIBS

2 racks St. Louis-style pork spare ribs

5 tsp (25 g) salt

14 dried ancho chiles, stemmed, seeded, dry roasted and rehydrated (page 18)

8 garlic cloves

1½ tsp (0.8 g) dried oregano, preferably Mexican

4 tsp (17 g) brown sugar

½ tsp ground cumin

2 tsp (10 g) ground black pepper

¼ cup (59 ml) olive oil

3½ cups (828 ml) water

1½ cups (355 ml) aged mezcal

CHIPOTLE-MOLASSES SAUCE

5 chipotles en adobo

1 tbsp (15 ml) dark molasses

3 tbsp (45 ml) sherry vinegar

2 tbsp (25 g) light brown sugar

2 tbsp (30 ml) agave nectar

½ cup (118 ml) water

2 tbsp (30 ml) soy sauce

1 tsp salt

OPTIONAL, FOR GARNISH

½ cup (20 g) cilantro leaves, chopped

MEZCAL-BRAISED RIBS

Rinse the ribs under cool water and pat dry with a paper towel. Remove the white membrane from the back of the ribs if your butcher has not done so already. Score any remaining membrane in a diamond pattern, being careful not to cut into the flesh of the rib. Generously rub the ribs with the salt and set aside while you prepare the rub.

Place the chiles, garlic, oregano, brown sugar, cumin and black pepper in a blender and blend to a fine puree. Lightly drizzle the ribs with olive oil and then thoroughly rub with the blended chile mixture. Let the ribs sit at room temperature for 1 hour, or refrigerated overnight.

Preheat the oven to 275°F (135°C).

Combine the water and mezcal and pour into the bottom of a roasting pan. Place a roasting rack in the pan, making sure that it's not touching the water–mezcal mixture. Place the ribs on the rack and cover tightly with two layers of aluminum foil. Cook in the preheated oven for 4½-5 hours, until the meat is extremely tender. Remove from the oven and allow the ribs to cool.

CHIPOTLE-MOLASSES SAUCE

Combine the chipotles, molasses, sherry vinegar, brown sugar, agave nectar, water and soy sauce in a blender and blending to a smooth puree. Place in a saucepan over medium-low heat and bring to a simmer for 10 minutes, until somewhat reduced and slightly thick. Remove from the heat, stir in the salt and set aside.

Preheat a grill or grill pan over medium heat.

If you are using a charcoal grill, light the fire and let the coals burn until they are covered with gray ash. Clean the grates and brush with a light coating of olive oil to prevent the ribs from sticking.

Cut the ribs into 6 bone segments to make them easier to work with. Place on the grill, brush with the Chipotle-Molasses Sauce and cook for 3-4 minutes, until slightly charred. Turn the ribs over, brush with more sauce and cook for an additional 3-4 minutes. Remove the ribs and place on a serving platter; sprinkle with chopped cilantro before serving, if desired.

Pierna de Puerco Adobada

ROASTED PORK LEG IN ADOBO SAUCE

When I was growing up, my mother would make a version of this dish that I absolutely loved. Even after I went away to college, this was the one item that I would ask her to make every visit home. Today, it is still a dish that tastes amazing to me and brings back so many wonderful memories.

The fresh ham is initially seasoned with a bright, citrus spice marinade and then slow roasted for hours in a sultry three-chile adobo sauce until tender. The final dish is topped with additional chile sauce to create a stylish main entrée bursting with flavor and perfect for any special dinner with family or friends.

YIELD: 12 SERVINGS

MARINADE

1 (10 lb [4.5 kg]) pork leg or fresh ham, outer rind and fat removed

8 garlic cloves, dry roasted (page 18)

½ large white onion, dry roasted (page 18)

4 bay leaves

1 tbsp (1.6 g) dried oregano, preferably Mexican

1 tsp black pepper

1 tsp ground cumin

½ cup (120 ml) fresh orange juice

½ cup (120 ml) apple cider vinegar

2 tsp (10 g) salt

ADOBO SAUCE

8 dried ancho chile peppers, stemmed, seeded, dry roasted and rehydrated (page 18)

6 dried pasilla chile peppers, stemmed, seeded, dry roasted and rehydrated (page 18)

2 dried guajillo chile peppers, stemmed, seeded, dry roasted and rehydrated (page 18)

2 cups (480 ml) fresh orange juice

1 cup (240 ml) apple cider vinegar

1 cup (240 ml) water

2 tbsp (30 g) salt

3 tbsp (45 ml) lard or canola oil

4 cups (960 ml) chicken broth

MARINADE

Rinse the pork under cool, running water and pat dry with a clean paper towel. Using a long knife, pierce the flesh 5–7 times to allow the marinade to easily penetrate.

In a blender, combine the garlic, onion, bay leaves, oregano, pepper, cumin, orange juice, vinegar and salt until thoroughly blended.

Place the pork in a large baking dish and thoroughly rub with the marinade. Cover and refrigerate for 4–8 hours.

ADOBO SAUCE

Add the rehydrated chiles to a blender along with the orange juice, vinegar, water and salt. Blend until smooth. Divide in half and set aside.

Preheat the oven to 350°F (177°C).

Remove the pork from the marinade and drizzle with the lard or canola oil. Use a pastry brush to coat the pork with half of the Adobo Sauce and place on a roasting rack in a large roasting pan. Pour the chicken broth around the pork and tightly cover with aluminum foil.

Cook the pork in the preheated oven for approximately 3 hours, or until the internal temperature reaches 160°F (71°C). Remove the pork from the roasting pan and place on a cutting board to cool slightly.

Pour the pan drippings along with the remaining half of the Adobo Sauce into a medium-size sauté pan and cook over medium heat for 10 minutes, until slightly reduced.

Slice the pork and place on a plate or serving platter and top with the reduced Adobo Sauce.

Cochinita Pibil

YUCATÁN ACHIOTE SEASONED PORK

Cochinita pibil is a traditional slow-roasted pork dish originating in the Yucatán region of Mexico. Cochinita literally means "baby pig," and the dish is often made in Mexico with a small, suckling pig. Since a whole pig is not always easy to find, I've created a version that utilizes my favorite pork cut—the shoulder. The flavors in this dish blend the intense acid of the citrus and vinegar with the earthy notes of the achiote and banana leaves. It is the ultimate flavor combination and something that I can make and eat again and again. Serve with Refried Black Beans (page 126) to create an amazing Yucatecán meal.

YIELD: 6 SERVINGS

1 (5–6 lb [2.3–2.7 kg]) pork shoulder, cut into 2"(5 cm) chunks

1½ tsp (4 g) black peppercorns

1 tsp cinnamon, preferably Mexican canela

1½ tsp (0.8 g) dried oregano, preferably Mexican

1 tsp cumin seeds

¼ tsp whole cloves

½ cup (120 ml) fresh orange juice

½ cup (120 ml) fresh lime juice

2 tsp (10 ml) white vinegar

4 oz (113 g) achiote paste

1 tbsp (15 g) salt

7 garlic cloves

1 package banana leaves, thawed

1 white onion, sliced

Tortillas, for serving

Yucatán Pickled Red Onions (page 120), for serving

Fiery Habanero Salsa (page 165), for serving

Rinse the pork shoulder under cool water and pat dry with a paper towel.

Grind the peppercorns, cinnamon, oregano, cumin seeds and whole cloves in a spice grinder until you have a fine puree. Place the ground spice mixture in a blender along with the orange juice, lime juice, vinegar, achiote paste, salt and garlic and puree until very smooth. Transfer the puree to a large mixing bowl or baking dish along with the pork. Toss to ensure that the pork is thoroughly coated. Refrigerate and marinate for 4 hours or up to overnight.

Preheat the oven to 350°F (177°C).

Cut 6 banana leaves to 1½ times the length of your roasting pan. Place the cut banana leaves in the pan with the sides overlapping. Pour the marinated pork on the banana leaves and top with the onion slices. Fold the banana leaves on top of the pork mixture. Seal tightly with two layers of aluminum foil and cook in the preheated oven for 2–3 hours until the pork is fork-tender.

Remove from the oven, discard the banana leaves and serve with the warm tortillas, red onions and salsa.

Note: You can make achiote paste yourself, or it can be found in most Latin markets or ordered online. Banana leaves are available in the frozen section of both Asian and Latin grocery stores.

Chiles en Nogada

STUFFED POBLANO CHILES WITH WALNUT SAUCE

Imagine a fire-roasted poblano pepper stuffed with ground meat and aromatic spices, smothered in a rich walnut sauce with sweet sherry and finally finished with a sprinkle of bright, tart pomegranate seeds. The completed dish is truly spectacular to both view and eat. In this dish, the flavors of the filling seem almost Moorish as they combine ground beef and pork with crisp, fresh and sweet, dried fruit. The slight heat of the roasted poblano pepper is perfectly balanced with the creamy walnut sauce. This recipe calls for the pepper to be battered and fried, but feel free to omit the frying and serve the stuffed pepper at room temperature without the golden fried batter.

YIELD: 12 SERVINGS

FILLING

3 tbsp (45 ml) lard or canola oil

1 small white onion, chopped

2 garlic cloves, minced

1 lb (454 g) ground pork

1 lb (454 g) ground beef

2 lb (907 g) Roma tomatoes, diced

3 small green apples, peeled, cored and chopped

3 pears, peeled, cored and chopped

½ cup (76 g) black raisins

½ cup (76 g) candied pineapple

½ cup (85 g) slivered almonds

½ cup (63 g) pine nuts

¼ tsp dried thyme

½ tsp dried oregano, preferably Mexican

½ tsp ground cinnamon

⅛ tsp ground cloves

Salt

12 poblano chile peppers, dry roasted, peeled and seeded (page 18)

WALNUT SAUCE

4 oz (113 g) walnuts, peeled

6 oz (170 g) cream cheese

1 cup (120 g) Mexican crema (page 15) or sour cream

½ cup (122 ml) milk

2 tbsp (30 ml) sherry

2 tbsp (24 g) sugar

Salt

CHILES

2 cups (480 ml) canola oil, for frying

1 cup (125 g) all-purpose flour

8 large eggs, separated

Salt

Fresh pomegranate seeds from 1 pomegranate

¼ cup (10 g) flat-leaf parsley, chopped

FILLING

Heat the lard in a large Dutch oven over medium-high heat until shimmering. Add the onion and cook for approximately 3–5 minutes, stirring often, until they're cooked through and translucent. Add the garlic and cook for an additional minute. Stir in the ground pork and beef and cook for approximately 10 minutes, stirring frequently, until the meat is almost cooked through. Add the diced tomatoes and cook for an additional 10 minutes, until the meat is thoroughly cooked and the tomatoes are tender.

Stir in the apples, pears, raisins, pineapple, almonds, pine nuts and spices. Turn the heat down to medium and slowly simmer the mixture, uncovered, for 30-40 minutes, until all the flavors are thoroughly blended and the liquid has evaporated. Season to taste with salt and set aside to cool. Once cool, place approximately ½ cup (118 g) of filling inside each chile and gently squeeze to close around the filling, forming a tight seal. Refrigerate until ready to fry.

WALNUT SAUCE

In a blender or food processor, puree the walnuts, cream cheese, crema and milk until smooth. Slowly drizzle the sherry into the mixture and continue blending for 1 minute until the sauce is extremely smooth. Add the sugar and salt to taste. Set aside.

CHILES

Heat the canola oil in a large sauté pan over medium-high heat. Meanwhile, place the flour in a shallow pan or baking dish and set aside. Beat the egg whites in a large bowl until soft peaks form. Whisk in the egg yolks and salt to taste. Working in batches, dredge each stuffed poblano chile in flour and lightly shake to remove any excess. Place each floured poblano in the egg batter and turn to ensure all sides are thoroughly coated.

Gently place a battered poblano in the oil and fry for approximately 4 minutes, until light brown. Gradually turn the chile over and cook the other side for an additional 3 minutes. Remove the chile pepper from the oil and place on a paper towel-lined tray to drain. Repeat the process with all of the peppers. Then, transfer the chiles to a serving platter and spoon the Walnut Sauce on top to thoroughly cover. Top with fresh pomegranate seeds and chopped parsley.

Albondigas Enchipotladas

MEXICAN MEATBALLS IN CHIPOTLE RED CHILE SAUCE

Albondigas are spicy Mexican meatballs traditionally served alone or in a soup. In this recipe, I've combined ground beef and pork with vibrant, flavorful garlic and cumin. The meatballs are baked in the oven in an intense Chipotle Red Chile Sauce. The roasting cooking method saves cooking time while also ensuring that the meatballs are moist and juicy.

The finished meatballs are topped with additional Chipotle Red Chile Sauce and garnished with tangy watercress and cotija cheese.

YIELD: 6 SERVINGS

CHIPOTLE RED CHILE SAUCE
10 Roma tomatoes, dry roasted (page 18)
4 garlic cloves, dry roasted and peeled (page 18)
5 chipotles en adobo
½ tsp ground cumin
1 tsp dried oregano, preferably Mexican
1 tsp salt
2 cups (480 ml) chicken broth

MEXICAN MEATBALLS
3 lb (1.4 kg) ground meat, 1½ lb (0.7 kg) beef and 1½ lb (0.7 kg) pork (or any combination)
1 tsp ground cumin
2 garlic cloves, dry roasted, peeled and minced (page 18)
2 tsp (10 g) salt
½ tsp black pepper
2 cups (118 g) breadcrumbs
4 large eggs
2 tbsp (30 ml) whole milk

GARNISH
Fresh watercress
Queso cotija
Chopped cilantro
Crusty bolillo rolls (optional)

Preheat the oven to 350°F (177°C).

CHIPOTLE RED CHILE SAUCE
Puree the tomatoes, garlic, chipotles, cumin, oregano, salt and chicken broth in a blender. Place the puree in a medium-size saucepan and simmer over medium heat for 5 minutes, until heated through and slightly thickened. Remove from the heat and pour half of the sauce into the bottom of a baking dish, setting the other half aside.

MEXICAN MEATBALLS
In a large mixing bowl, combine the ground meat, cumin, garlic, salt and pepper. Using your hands, stir in the breadcrumbs, eggs and milk until thoroughly combined. Form the mixture into 2-ounce (57 g) meatballs approximately 3 inches (7.6 cm) in diameter and place in the prepared baking dish with the sauce. Repeat with the remaining meat mixture.

Pour the remaining half of the Chipotle Red Chile Sauce on top of the meatballs and tightly cover with a double layer of aluminum foil. Cook in the preheated oven for 30–40 minutes, until the meatballs are completely cooked through.

Remove from the oven and serve on plates or a serving platter. Garnish with the fresh watercress, queso cotija and chopped cilantro and serve with the bolillo rolls, if desired.

Ancho Filete con Champinones

ANCHO-RUBBED BEEF TENDERLOIN FILLETS WITH WILD MUSHROOM-CHIPOTLE SAUCE

Growing up in Oklahoman cattle country, I can't ignore my absolute love for a great steak. This recipe is a variation of a dish prepared in Chihuahua, Mexico, and an absolute favorite of mine.

Beef tenderloin is typically not a flavorful cut of beef, so the secret of this dish lies in the sauce, which combines the earthiness of wild mushrooms with the smoky spiciness of chipotle peppers. The addition of the creamy, melted cheese at the end lends an element of surprise and helps balance out the bold spice of the sauce.

The final dish makes an elegant and memorable entrée for any special occasion or special person.

YIELD: 6 SERVINGS

CHIPOTLE SAUCE
2 garlic cloves, dry roasted, peeled and roughly chopped (page 18)

2 chipotles en adobo, finely chopped

2 dried ancho chile peppers, dry roasted, stemmed, seeded and rehydrated (page 18)

½ tsp dried oregano, preferably Mexican

⅛ tsp ground cloves

1–1½ cup (240–360 ml) chicken broth

2 tbsp (30 ml) agave syrup

¾ tsp salt

ANCHO CHILE RUB
½ cup (58 g) ancho chile powder

2 tsp (5 g) chile de árbol powder

2 tsp (10 g) ground black pepper

½ cup (100 g) light brown sugar

2 tbsp (30 g) salt

TENDERLOIN FILLET
6–8 oz (170–227 g) center-cut beef tenderloin fillets

2 tbsp (30 ml) olive oil

4 slices Chihuahua or Monterey Jack cheese

1 tbsp (15 g) unsalted butter

2 cups (133 g) (cut ½" [13 mm]-thick) assorted wild mushrooms

2 cups (480 ml) red wine

1 tsp salt

1 tbsp (3 g) cilantro leaves, chopped

CHIPOTLE SAUCE
Puree all of the ingredients in a blender until smooth. Taste and season with any additional salt, if desired. Set aside.

ANCHO CHILE RUB
Thoroughly combine all of the ingredients in a large bowl.

TENDERLOIN FILLET
Generously rub each of the tenderloin fillets with the rub. Heat the oil in a large sauté pan over medium-high heat. Cook the seasoned tenderloins for approximately 3 minutes, turn over, top with a slice of cheese and cook for an additional 3 minutes, or until the internal temperature is 130°F (54°C) for medium-rare. Transfer the cooked tenderloins to a wire rack or baking sheet and let rest for 5 minutes.

Add the butter and the mushrooms to the drippings in the pan used to cook the tenderloins and sauté for 1 minute. Add the red wine and the Chipotle Sauce and cook for an additional 3 minutes, until slightly reduced and the mushrooms are tender. Season with salt.

Transfer each tenderloin to a plate and top with the mushroom sauce. Garnish with the chopped cilantro and serve immediately.

Carne Asada Roja

RED CHILE-MARINATED RIB EYE STEAKS

In Mexico this dish would typically utilize a flank or thinner steak, but I created this version using a rib eye because I love its flavor. The thick, fatty rib eye easily retains the intense garlicky flavor of the marinade and chars beautifully on the grill. Warm Salsa Roja makes the perfect finishing element to add a touch of essential acidity and saltiness to the dish. Serve it alongside Spicy Bacon Pinto Beans (page 128) and topped with fresh cilantro.

YIELD: 6 SERVINGS

16 guajillo chiles, stemmed, seeded, dry roasted and rehydrated (page 18)

5 garlic cloves, dry roasted and peeled (page 18)

2 tsp (7 g) cumin seeds

½ tbsp (0.8 g) dried oregano, preferably Mexican

1 tbsp (15 ml) cider vinegar

3 cups (720 ml) vegetable or chicken broth

1 tsp canola oil

1 tbsp (15 g) salt

1 tbsp (12 g) sugar

6 (12 oz [340 g]) 1" (2.5 cm)-thick boneless rib eye steaks

Olive oil, for grill

Sliced avacados

1 cup (240 ml) Salsa Roja (page 154), warm

Puree the rehydrated chiles, garlic, cumin, oregano, vinegar and 1 cup (240 ml) of the broth in a blender for 5 minutes, until extremely smooth.

Heat the canola oil in heavy-bottomed saucepan over medium-high heat. Once the oil is hot and begins to shimmer, pour the pureed chile mixture into the pan. Be careful, as the sauce will splatter. Immediately stir and reduce the heat to medium-low. Simmer, stirring often, for 10 minutes, until the sauce thickens and begins to darken.

Stir in the remaining 2 cups (480 ml) broth along with the salt and sugar. Continue to simmer for an additional 20 minutes to reduce. Remove the mixture from the heat and season with additional salt if desired. Transfer to a large, shallow baking dish and set aside to cool completely prior to marinating the steak.

Place the steaks in the red chile marinade, making sure that the pieces are thoroughly coated. Cover and refrigerate for a minimum of 4 hours, or overnight.

Preheat an outdoor grill or grill pan over medium-high heat. Lightly brush the grill grates with olive oil to prevent the steaks from sticking. Place the steaks on the grill and cook for approximately 12 minutes for medium-rare steaks, turning once.

Allow the steaks to rest for 5 minutes before serving.

Serve with the sliced avocado and topped with the warm Salsa Roja.

Costillas de Borrego con Mole Coloradito

PUMPKIN SEED–CRUSTED RACK OF LAMB WITH OAXACAN RED MOLE SAUCE

Mexican moles differ from family to family and from state to state. This red mole sauce, originating in the Mexican state of Oaxaca, is completely different than any other. It has the same deep, intense flavors of the Mole Poblano but with a brighter taste. Drizzled atop the herbaceous pumpkin seed–crusted lamb, it helps create a truly memorable dish.

YIELD: 4 SERVINGS

OAXACAN RED MOLE

8 dried ancho chile peppers, stemmed, seeded, dry roasted and rehydrated (page 18)

8 guajillo chile peppers, stemmed, seeded, dry roasted and rehydrated (page 18)

5 cups (1.2 L) chicken broth

1 tbsp (10 g) sesame seeds

5 whole black peppercorns

3 whole cloves

½ tsp dried oregano, preferably Mexican

1 tsp ground cinnamon or Mexican canela

3 garlic cloves, dry roasted and peeled (page 18)

6 Roma tomatoes, dry roasted (page 18)

2 tbsp (30 ml) lard or canola oil

½ cup (96 g) sugar

1½ oz (43 g) Mexican chocolate

1 tsp salt

PUMPKIN SEED CRUST

1 tbsp (15 ml) canola oil

4 garlic cloves, minced

1 cup (63 g) shelled pumpkin seeds

LAMB

1 tbsp (15 ml) canola oil

2 (1½ lb [680 g]) 8-rib Frenched racks of lamb, trimmed of all but a thin layer of fat

1½ tsp (8 g) salt

¾ tsp black pepper

½ cup (120 ml) agave syrup

OAXACAN RED MOLE

Place the rehydrated guajillo and ancho chiles in a blender along with 1 cup (240 ml) of the chicken broth and thoroughly blend. If necessary, add up to 1 additional cup (240 ml) of the broth to form a very smooth puree. Strain the mixture through a fine-mesh strainer, pressing hard to extract as much liquid as possible. Discard the large particles (there should be less than ¼ cup [59 ml] of large particles left in the strainer) and set aside.

Heat a large cast-iron pan or comal over medium-high heat. Once the pan is very hot, toast the sesame seeds for 1–2 minutes, until just golden brown. Remove the sesame seeds from the pan and place in the bowl of a blender. Return the pan or comal to the heat and seperately toast the peppercorns, cloves, dried oregano and cinnamon for 1–2 minutes each.

Add the roasted garlic and tomatoes to the blender along with the toasted spices and seasame seeds. Blend the mixture, adding up to 1 cup (240 ml) of the chicken broth if necessary to form a smooth puree. Strain the mixture through a fine-mesh strainer, pressing hard to extract as much liquid as possible. Discard the large particles.

Heat the lard or canola oil in a saucepan over medium heat. Once the oil is hot, but not smoking, add the pureed chile mixture to the pan. Stir and cook for 10 minutes, until it changes color and begins to thicken. Reduce the heat to medium-low and add the garlic-spice puree to the pan; stir to blend. Add the remaining 2 cups (480 ml) chicken broth and simmer for 20 minutes, stirring often.

Add the sugar and chocolate to the mixture and simmer for an additional 20 minutes, stirring often, until the mixture thickens and coats the back of a spoon when stirred. Season with salt, adding more to taste if desired. Keep warm.

Preheat the oven to 350°F (177°C).

PUMPKIN SEED CRUST

Heat the oil in a large sauté pan over medium heat until the oil shimmers. Stir the minced garlic into the pan and cook for 1–2 minutes, until the garlic begins to turn a light golden brown. Add the pumpkin seeds and cook for an addition 2–3 minutes, stirring often, until the seeds are lightly toasted. Transfer the mixture to a blender or food processor and pulse until coarse.

LAMB

Raise the heat to medium-high and heat the canola oil in the pan until it shimmers. Rinse the lamb under cool water and pat dry with a clean paper towel. Season with salt and pepper and place in the hot skillet (in 2 batches, if necessary); cook for 4–6 minutes, until all sides are golden brown.

Remove the lamb from the heat and transfer to a roasting pan. Spread the agave over the round side of the lamb and press half of the Pumpkin Seed Crust onto each rack. Roast in the preheated oven for approximately 10–12 minutes, or until a thermometer registers 130°F (54°C) for medium-rare. Then, cut each rack into 4 double chops. Spoon some of the mole sauce onto the center of each plate and top with 2 of the double chops. Serve immediately.

Barbacoa de Borrego

MEXICAN BARBECUED LAMB

In Mexico, the barbacoa style of cooking varies by region, but it typically refers to meat that is slow-roasted for hours in a pit or over an open fire. In my rendition of the traditional Barbacoa de Borrego, lamb shoulder is rubbed with a chile-spiced adobo, wrapped in banana leaves and then slow-roasted in the oven for hours.

The secret to this dish relies not only on the balanced acidity and piquancy of the adobo but also on cooking the lamb for a long period of time at a low temperature. The end result is a perfect blend of rich, juicy lamb and strong, aromatic spices.

YIELD: 12 SERVINGS

ADOBO RUB

6 garlic cloves, dry roasted and peeled (page 18)

6 dried ancho chiles, stemmed, seeded, dry roasted and rehydrated (page 18)

6 guajillo chiles, stemmed, seeded, dry roasted and rehydrated (page 18)

⅓ cup (79 ml) apple cider vinegar

1 tbsp (1.6 g) dried oregano, preferably Mexican

1 tsp cinnamon

5 whole cloves

1 tsp sugar

4 tsp (20 g) salt

1 cup (240 ml) water, as needed

2 tbsp (30 ml) canola oil

LAMB

1 (6–8 lb [2.7–3.6 kg]) bone-in lamb shoulder, fat and silver skin removed

3–4 cups (700–950 ml) water

1 (1 lb [450 g]) package banana leaves, thawed

1 small white onion, sliced

6 oz (170 g) avocado leaves, crumbled

Tortillas, for serving

Roasted Tomatillo Salsa (page 157)

ADOBO RUB

Blend the garlic, rehydrated ancho and guajillo chiles, vinegar, oregano, cinnamon, cloves, sugar and salt in a blender to form a thick paste. If necessary, add up to 1 cup (240 ml) of water to the blender for the mixture to blend smoothly.

Heat the canola oil in a medium-size saucepan over medium-high heat. When the oil is very hot and begins to shimmer, add the blended paste to the pan and immediately stir. Be careful, as the paste will splatter. Fry for 4–5 minutes, stirring constantly, until it thickens and begins to darken. Remove from the heat and cool to room temperature before using.

LAMB

Rinse the lamb under cool water and pat dry with a clean paper towel. Thoroughly rub the lamb with the Adobo Rub and marinate in the refrigerator for 4–12 hours.

Preheat the oven to 300°F (149°C).

Place a roasting rack in a baking pan and pour the water in the bottom of the pan, making sure the water does not reach the roasting rack.

Cut 6 banana leaves to 1½ times the length of your roasting pan. Place the leaves in the pan with their sides overlapping. Add the lamb to the pan, sprinkle with the sliced onions and avocado leaves and fold the banana leaves over so that the lamb is completely encased inside them. Cover the pan with aluminum foil and roast in the preheated oven for approximately 4 hours, until the lamb is extremely tender.

Remove from the oven and use 2 forks to shred the lamb into thin strands. Pour any pan drippings on top of the lamb and serve with the warm tortillas and salsa.

Note: In Mexico, it is a common tradition to bury a bottle of mezcal or tequila along with the meat and raise the bottle from the pit, serve and toast to the feast. Why not create your own version of the tradition by enjoying a rich glass of Herradura Anejo or mezcal just prior to the meal? *Salud!*

four

Pescado y Mariscos

FISH AND SEAFOOD

Living on the coast of New England, seafood is readily available. That is probably the reason that this chapter is the longest in the book.

The chapter begins with ceviche, which is one of my absolute favorite things to eat. My first taste of ceviche was sitting on a restaurant deck in Baja, Mexico, overlooking the ocean. The warm Mexican sun along with the distinct restaurant smells helped create a memory that I will never forget.

Growing up in a small town in southwestern Oklahoma, I have never seen marinated fish and I was a bit squeamish to say the least. Those fears were quickly erased as I took my first bite. The lime-marinated fish was like nothing I had ever had before and it seemed to almost melt in my mouth. I was hooked from the very first taste, and now whenever I see ceviche on a restaurant menu, I quickly order it before the server can even ask for my drink selection.

At my restaurants, we serve a variety of ceviches. The abundance of fresh seafood in New England allows us to travel to local fish markets that have a huge selection of fresh fish to choose from. It's like heaven for the ceviche lover.

When I prepare ceviche for my guests or work to create a new ceviche recipe, I am making those memories fresh again and once again remembering the smells and flavors of my first bite of ceviche that wonderful day in Mexico.

Note: For any of the dishes in this chapter, I strongly suggest buying and using the freshest seafood possible. Don't be afraid to be particular with your selection. Ask your fishmonger where it is from and smell the fish. It should have a seafood smell of the ocean and not an overly fishy odor.

Ceviche a la Veracruzano

CLASSIC VERACRUZ-STYLE CEVICHE

Fresh ceviche is a true masterpiece of Mexican cuisine. The subtle flavors of marinated white fish combined with the lively acidity of the lime is amazingly refreshing, especially on a hot summer day.

In this version, originating in the state of Veracruz, fresh fish is marinated in lime and then combined with tomato juice, plump olives and spicy serrano chile to create a bold, flavorful dish with an almost Mediterranean flavor. You can serve this dish as an appetizer or atop fresh greens to make a beautiful ceviche salad. Ceviche a la Veracruzano pairs amazingly well with a light Mexican beer or, if you are a tequila drinker, try it with a silver tequila such as Herradura.

YIELD: 4 SERVINGS

1 lb (450 g) very fresh, firm-flesh fish (I prefer halibut or red snapper), cut into ½" (13 mm) dice

½ cup (76 g) finely diced white onion

1 cup (240 ml) lime juice, preferably freshly squeezed

1 cup (240 ml) tomato juice

1 tbsp (2.5 g) fresh cilantro leaves, chopped

2 tbsp (30 ml) olive oil

2 Roma tomatoes, finely diced

2 serrano chiles, finely diced

½ cup (90 g) green Manzanilla olives, halved

¼ tsp salt

1 ripe avocado, cut into slices

Tortilla chips, for serving

Place the diced fish and onion in a large glass bowl and top with the lime juice. Cover the bowl and marinate in the refrigerator for 4 hours, until the fish is completely opaque. Remove from the refrigerator, drain and discard the lime juice.

Gently stir the tomato juice, chopped cilantro, olive oil, tomatoes, chile, olives and salt into the fish and onion mixture. Taste and season with additional salt if necessary.

Top with avocado slices and serve with warm tortilla chips.

Note: Ceviche is the method of preparing seafood where the acid "cooks" (or actually breaks down the protein in) the seafood in place of heat.

Ceviche de Vieiras

SCALLOP CEVICHE WITH GINGER-SERRANO SALSA

This ceviche has a slight Asian flavor and combines the freshness of basil and the spice of serrano chile peppers with thinly sliced orange-marinated scallops. It is finished with a tangy ginger salsa and a light drizzle of fragrant olive oil. You can serve it with fresh tortilla chips or eat it by itself (as I do). Be sure to slice the scallops very thinly and marinate until they are "cooked" through and completely opaque.

YIELD: 6 SERVINGS

10 (1 lb [454 g]) extra-large (U/10) scallops, cut crosswise 4 times to form 4 large coins per scallop (40 total)

Juice and zest of 2 oranges (kept separate)

GINGER-SERRANO SALSA
1 tbsp (14 g) finely diced ginger
1 tbsp (15 g) finely diced shallot
2 serrano chiles, finely diced
1 tbsp (15 ml) oyster sauce
2 tbsp (30 ml) sherry vinegar
1 tbsp (15 ml) soy sauce
½ tsp lime juice

½ cup (20 g) basil, sliced into thin strips (chiffonade)
½ cup (120 ml) olive oil
Tortilla chips (optional)

Place the scallops in a large glass bowl and cover with the orange juice. Thoroughly toss the scallops to ensure that all pieces are thoroughly covered. Marinate for 1 hour, or until the scallops are completely opaque. Drain and discard the orange juice.

GINGER-SERRANO SALSA
Stir together the ginger, shallot, serrano chiles, oyster sauce, vinegar, soy sauce and lime juice. Set aside.

Toss the basil, olive oil and orange zest with the marinated scallops. Spoon onto a serving platter or into a serving glass and drizzle with the Ginger-Serrano Salsa. Serve with fresh tortilla chips, if desired.

Ceviche de Langosta

LOBSTER GUAVA CEVICHE

This is an elegant version of ceviche that replaces the typical lime-marinated fish with steamed, buttery Maine lobster. The succulent lobster goes amazingly well with the sweetness of the guava and thanks to the diced tomato, crisp onions and scallions, you get a variety of flavors and textures in every bite. The final addition of tart grapefruit creates an unexpected "wow" factor. Serve it in clear martini glasses to add to the stunning visual appeal of this dish.

This dish is surprisingly simple to prepare, but if you want to make it even easier, you can purchase prepared lobster meat (if your grocer prepares it fresh). Stay away from prepackaged meat that has been frozen, as the fresh texture and flavor of lobster is essential in this dish.

Guava juice is available at most well-stocked grocery and Latin markets. If you can't find it, feel free to substitute mango, passion fruit or even pineapple juice.

YIELD: 4 SERVINGS

1 mango, peeled and seeded

1 small red onion, julienned

3 Roma tomatoes, diced

2 scallions, sliced crosswise

2 tbsp (30 ml) lime juice

2 cups (480 ml) guava juice (I prefer the brand Goya)

1 tsp salt

2 lb (907 g) Maine lobster meat, steamed and cut into bite-size pieces (keep the claws, if available, for garnish)

4 tsp (3.4 g) cilantro leaves, chopped

1 grapefruit, segmented and roughly chopped

Tortilla chips, for serving

Place the fresh mango in a blender and puree for 2 minutes, or until completely smooth. Remove from the blender and place in a large glass bowl along with the onion, tomatoes, scallions, lime juice, guava juice and salt. Stir the chopped lobster into the mixture.

Spoon the lobster ceviche onto a serving platter or individual serving glasses and top with chopped cilantro and grapefruit. Garnish with the lobster claws, if available. Serve with fresh tortilla chips.

Note: In Mexico, lobsters are an important commercial resource. The lobsters available throughout Mexico are primarily spiny lobsters, which have a milder flavor than the Maine lobster seen throughout the US. I've created this version using the Maine lobster that is so abundant where I live, but you can substitute spiny lobster if that is more readily available to you.

Coctel de Calamares y Camarones

SHRIMP AND SQUID COCKTAIL

If you are a bit timid to try typical ceviche, which marinates raw fish in lime juice, this dish is an excellent option. In this cocktail, the shrimp and squid are slightly cooked and then added to the citrus prior to serving. The end result is just as refreshing and delicious as classic ceviche.

YIELD: 8 SERVINGS

1 lb (454 g) raw squid

1 lb (454 g) medium shrimp, cleaned, deveined, and tails removed

1 lime, quartered

1 bay leaf

½ cup (120 ml) orange juice

½ cup (120 ml) lime juice

½ habanero chile, finely diced

1 tbsp (15 ml) agave nectar

1 tsp salt

1 orange, segmented and cut into small, bite-size chunks

½ cup (80 g) peeled and thinly sliced cucumber

½ cup (90 g) peeled and thinly sliced jicama

¼ cup (32.5 g) thinly sliced red onion

¼ cup (10 g) cilantro leaves, finely chopped

Tortilla chips, for serving

Rinse the squid and the shrimp (separately) under cool water.

Slice the squid crosswise into $\frac{1}{3}$-inch (8.5 mm)-thick rings. If you are using the tentacles, cut them into large bite-size pieces, remembering that they will shrink slightly when cooked. Place the cleaned squid in a medium-size colander. Add 2–3 inches (5–7.6 cm) of water to a large stockpot along with the lime and bay leaf and bring to a boil over medium heat. Set the colander with the squid inside the pot.

Cover the pot and simmer for 2 minutes. Remove the lid and gently stir the squid so that it cooks evenly, cover and steam for another 1 minute, until the squid is completely cooked through. Remove the colander from the pot and pour the squid into a bowl filled with ice to immediately stop the cooking process and cool the squid.

Place the shrimp in the colander and set the colander back into the pot; cover and simmer for 2 minutes. Remove the lid and gently stir the shrimp to cook evenly. Cover and steam for another 2 minutes, until the shrimp are completely cooked and begin to form a "C" shape.

Remove the colander from the pot and place in a sink. Pour the bowl with the squid and ice on top of the shrimp to immediately stop the cooking process. Add additional ice if the majority of what was in the bowl has melted. Set aside to cool and drain. Lightly rinse the mixture under cool water to ensure that no ice is left prior to combining with the remaining ingredients.

In a large glass bowl, combine the orange juice, lime juice, habanero, agave nectar and salt. Stir in the orange segments, cucumber, jicama, red onion, shrimp and squid. Sprinkle with chopped cilantro and serve with fresh tortilla chips.

Note: This seafood cocktail combines cooked shrimp and squid. Feel free to use a combination of the two or omit one if desired.

Ceviche de Atun

TUNA AND WATERMELON CEVICHE

In open markets in Mexico, succulent watermelon mingles beside other local fruits. The combination and textural difference of watermelon and fresh tuna is fantastic and works so well in this dish. Try it alone or atop a crisp tostada.

YIELD: 4 SERVINGS

1 lb (454 g) sashimi-grade tuna, cut into ½" (13 mm) dice

2½ cups (420 g), ½" (13 mm) diced, seedless watermelon

Juice of 2 limes

½ habanero chile, finely diced

2 tbsp (25 g) finely diced white onion

2 tbsp (30 ml) olive oil

2 tbsp (5 g) cilantro leaves, finely chopped

Tortilla chips, for serving

In a medium-size glass bowl, combine the tuna, watermelon, lime juice, habanero, onion and olive oil. Stir to thoroughly combine the ceviche. Sprinkle with chopped cilantro and serve in individual glass bowls or skewered alongside fresh tortilla chips.

Note: If you want to further intensify the watermelon flavor, pair it with a Watermelon Habanero Margarita (page 176).

Ceviche de Pulpo

OCTOPUS CEVICHE

Throughout Mexico, you can find countless varieties of ceviche. Although I love all versions, my favorite has always been octopus. If you've never eaten octopus, don't let it intimidate you. The flavor is very mellow and surprisingly similar to squid, with a much meatier texture. In this recipe, the flavor of the octopus is intensified with the addition of habanero, ginger and citrus, while soy sauce mimics the flavor of the ocean with just a hint of briny saltiness.

YIELD: 4 SERVINGS

1 cup (240 ml) lemon juice

½ cup (120 ml) orange juice

2 tsp (10 g) salt

4 tsp (20 ml) soy sauce

2 garlic cloves, grated

2 tsp (10 g) grated ginger

1 habanero chile, finely diced

1 lb (454 g) octopus

1 tsp salt

1 white onion, quartered

1 bay leaf

¼ cup (32.5 g) thinly sliced red onion

½ cup (80 g) quartered grape or cherry tomatoes

¼ cup (10 g) cilantro leaves, chopped

In a large glass bowl, combine the lemon juice, orange juice, salt, soy sauce, garlic, ginger and habanero chile. Set aside and chill until ready to use.

Wash the octopus under cool water and thoroughly rub with salt.

Place approximately 6 inches (15 cm) of water in a pressure cooker along with the onion and bay leaf. Bring the mixture to a boil and place a vegetable steamer in the pot over the water. Gently place the octopus in the steamer basket and close the pressure cooker lid. Steam for approximately 30 minutes. Release the pressure in the pot and allow the cooker to cool prior to opening.

Remove the octopus from the pot and cool in an ice bath. Once cool enough to handle, remove the octopus from the ice bath and slice into ⅛"-(3 mm)-thick medallions.

Place the octopus medallions into the ceviche mixture and stir in the red onion, tomatoes and chopped cilantro. Chill until ready to serve.

Note: Octopus can be found at local gourmet grocery and Asian markets. Don't be afraid to purchase frozen octopus as the freezing process helps tenderize the meat. If purchased frozen, thaw before cooking.

Rellenos de Camarones

SHRIMP-STUFFED POBLANO CHILE PEPPERS WITH GREEN CHILE CREAM SAUCE

The poblano chile originates from the Mexican state of Pueblo, and it's typically a very mild pepper. There are many versions of stuffed poblanos available throughout Mexico. My version intensifies the smoky flavor that the poblanos have once they are roasted by combining them with smoky chipotle-spiced shrimp. The slightly spicy and tangy Green Chile Cream Sauce further adds to the bold flavor.

YIELD: 4 SERVINGS

GREEN CHILE CREAM SAUCE

3 poblano chiles, dry roasted, stemmed, seeded and peeled (page 18)

¼ white onion, dry roasted (page 18)

1 garlic clove, dry roasted and peeled (page 18)

¾ cup (90.5 g) Mexican crema (page 15)

¾ cup (177 ml) half-and-half

1 tsp dried oregano, preferably Mexican

½ tsp salt

CHIPOTLE-SPICED SHRIMP

2 tbsp (30 ml) olive oil

2 garlic cloves, minced

1 chipotle chile en adobo

¼ tsp dried oregano, preferably Mexican

1 lb (454 g) medium to large shrimp, peeled, deveined and tails removed

2 tbsp (29 g) unsalted butter

½ tsp salt

4 poblano chiles, dry roasted, stemmed, seeded and peeled (page 18)

½ cup (65 g) shredded Monterey Jack cheese

¼ cup (10 g) cilantro leaves, chopped

GREEN CHILE CREAM SAUCE

Place the dry roasted poblano peppers, onion, garlic, Mexican crema, half-and-half, dried oregano and salt in a blender or food processor. Puree for 2 minutes, or until extremely smooth. Taste and season with additional salt, if necessary. Heat the sauce in a medium saucepan over medium heat until it begins to steam and is warmed through. Do not bring the sauce to a boil or simmer.

CHIPOTLE-SPICED SHRIMP

In a blender or food processor, puree the olive oil, minced garlic, chipotle chile en adobo and oregano until extremely smooth. Place in a large bowl along with the shrimp. Toss to combine the mixture and ensure that the shrimp are completely covered. Set aside to marinate in the refrigerator for 20–30 minutes.

Heat the butter in a large sauté pan over medium heat until shimmering. Add the marinated shrimp all at once, being careful as it will splatter, and cook for 3–4 minutes, until the shrimp are just beginning to form a "C" shape. They do not need to be completely done as they will finish the cooking process in the oven. Season with the salt.

Preheat the oven to 350°F (177°C).

Add approximately ½ cup (165 g) of Chipotle-Spiced Shrimp inside each poblano chile, top with a spoonful of cheese and gently squeeze the chile to close around the filling and form a tight seal. Place on a baking sheet, seam side up, and repeat the process with the remaining chiles.

Place the baking dish in the oven and heat for 6–8 minutes, or until heated through and the cheese has melted. Serve on a plate and top with the warm Green Chile Cream Sauce and sprinkle with the chopped cilantro.

Note: This recipe calls for 1 chipotle chile en adobo found canned in the Latin section of your local grocery store. The remaining chiles can be stored, tightly covered, in your refrigerator for up to 2 weeks.

Mariscos de Campechana

MIXED SEAFOOD COCKTAIL

This is a classic dish from the state of Campeche along the Gulf of Mexico. It is a seafood lover's dream, as it is packed full of a variety of seafood, including succulent raw oysters.

The addition of ketchup may seem a bit unusual, but it is used throughout Mexico as an accompaniment to ceviches and seafood cocktails and further enhances the slight sweetness of the shrimp. The addition of chipotle adds a nice balance of heat to the dish.

In this recipe, I've used shrimp, octopus, crab and raw oysters, but feel free to use more or less of one type of seafood or omit one altogether.

YIELD: 6 SERVINGS

½ lb (227 g) medium-size shrimp, peeled, deveined and tails removed

½ lb (227 g) octopus

2 tsp (10 g) salt

1 lime, quartered

1 bay leaf

½ cup (110 g) ketchup

1 tbsp (11 g) finely chopped chipotle en adobo

¼ cup (10 g) cilantro leaves, chopped

2 tbsp (30 ml) olive oil

½ small white onion, chopped

4 Roma tomatoes, diced

2 serrano chiles, finely chopped

12 fresh oysters, shucked

½ lb (227 g) crabmeat, jumbo lump

Juice of 1 lime

1 avocado, peeled, pitted and sliced

Tortilla chips, for serving

Rinse the shrimp and octopus (separately) under cool water. Rub the octopus with 1 teaspoon of the salt and place in a medium-size colander.

Add 3-4 inches (7.6-10 cm) of water to a large pot along with the lime and bay leaf and bring to a boil over medium heat. Set the colander with the octopus inside the pot, cover and simmer for 30 minutes, until the octopus is extremely tender and practically falling off of the fork. Make sure that you check the octopus every 5-7 minutes to ensure the water has not boiled away. Remove the colander from the pot and pour the octopus into a bowl filled with ice to immediately stop the cooking process and cool the octopus. Once cool, slice the octopus into ¼-inch (6 mm)-thick medallions.

Place the shrimp in the colander and set the colander into a pot with 3-4 inches (7.6-10 cm) of boiling water. Cover the pot and simmer for 2 minutes. Remove the lid and gently stir the shrimp so that they will cook evenly. Cover and steam for another 2 minutes, until the shrimp are completely cooked through and begin to form a "C" shape. Remove the colander from the pot and pour the shrimp into a bowl filled with ice. Lightly rinse the mixture under cool water to ensure that there is no ice left prior to combining with the remaining ingredients.

In a large glass bowl, combine the ketchup, chipotle en adobo, cilantro, olive oil, onion, diced tomatoes, serrano chiles and remaining 1 teaspoon salt. Stir the octopus, shrimp, oysters and crab into the mixture. Drizzle with a squeeze of lime. Taste and season with additional salt, if necessary. Top with fresh avocado slices and serve with warm tortilla chips.

Pescado con Pipian Verde

CILANTRO-MARINATED HALIBUT WITH GREEN PUMPKIN SEED SAUCE

Pipian Verde is a wonderful traditional Mexican sauce made with serrano chiles, tomatillos and pumpkin seeds. It has an intense nutty, earthy flavor and although technically a mole, it is surprisingly simple to make. The Cilantro Marinade adds a touch of acidity and a nice herbaceous quality to the fish. I've used halibut here, but you can easily substitute any hearty fish, such as fluke, flounder or cod. The sauce can even be prepared ahead of time with just a final sauté of the fish prior to serving.

YIELD: 4 SERVINGS

CILANTRO MARINADE
2 cups (80 g) cilantro, stems intact
1 cup (240 ml) extra virgin olive oil
1 tbsp (15 ml) lime juice
¼ tsp salt

4 (6 oz [170 g]) halibut fillets

PIPIAN VERDE
5–6 tomatillos
2 serrano chile peppers, dry roasted (page 18)
2 garlic cloves, dry roasted and peeled (page 18)
½ medium white onion, dry roasted (page 18)
½ cup (20 g) fresh cilantro leaves
2 romaine lettuce leaves
¾ cup (90 g) pumpkin seeds
¼ cup (40 g) raw unsalted peanuts
2 tbsp (20 g) sesame seeds
2 tbsp (30 ml) canola oil
Salt

2 tbsp (30 ml) olive oil
¼ cup (31 g) all-purpose flour
½ tsp salt
⅛ tsp black pepper

OPTIONAL, FOR GARNISH
Pumpkin seeds
Cilantro

CILANTRO MARINADE
Bring 6 cups (1.4 L) of water to a simmer in a medium-size saucepan over high heat. Quickly blanch the cilantro by dropping it into the water for 20 seconds; remove with a slotted spoon. Cool the cilantro under running water and pat dry with paper towels. Add the blanched cilantro to a blender along with the extra virgin olive oil, lime juice and salt. Blend to a smooth puree. Pour the mixture into a glass baking dish or large shallow bowl. Pat the fish fillets dry with a clean paper towel and place in the dish with the marinade. Liberally spoon additional marinade over the fish to ensure that the fillets are completely covered. Place the fish and marinade in the refrigerator for 1 hour, and up to 3 hours.

PIPIAN VERDE
Place the tomatillos in a 4-quart (4 L) heavy-bottomed saucepan and covering them completely with water. Place the pan over medium-high heat and bring to a boil for 4–5 minutes, or until the tomatillos are just tender. Using a slotted spoon, remove the tomatillos from the pan and add to a blender along with 2 cups (480 ml) of the reserved tomatillo cooking liquid, serrano chiles, garlic, onion, cilantro and romaine. Puree for 3 minutes, or until smooth. Pour the puree through a fine-mesh strainer and discard any large particles.

Heat a small sauté or cast-iron pan over medium-high heat. Once the pan is hot, add the pumpkin seeds and peanuts and lightly toast for 2 minutes until fragrant. Transfer the seeds and peanuts to a blender. Return the same pan to the heat and lightly toast the sesame seeds for 1 minute, or until just golden. Transfer the toasted sesame seeds to the blender along with 2 cups (480 ml) of the reserved tomatillo cooking liquid. Puree for 3 minutes, until smooth. Pour the puree through a fine-mesh strainer and discard any large particles.

Heat the canola oil in a saucepan over medium-high heat. When the oil is very hot and begins to shimmer, pour the pureed vegetable sauce into the pan and immediately stir. Be careful as the sauce will splatter. Fry the sauce for 2–3 minutes, stirring constantly, until the sauce thickens and begins to darken. Stir in the pureed pumpkin seed mixture and cook for an additional 5 minutes, until the sauce further thickens. Season to taste with salt.

Heat the olive oil in a sauté pan over medium-high heat until hot.

Add the flour to a shallow baking dish. Remove the fish from the marinade and lightly dredge both sides in the flour mixture. Gently shake to remove excess and season both sides liberally with salt and pepper. Place the fish into the pan, skin side down, and cook for 4 minutes, until nicely browned on the bottom. Gently turn the fish over and cook the other side for an additional 3–4 minutes, or until the fish is cooked through and begins to flake. Place the fish on a plate or serving platter and top with the Pipian Verde sauce. Garnish with pumpkin seeds and a sprig of cilantro, if desired.

Note: At the restaurants, we strain the Pipian Verde multiple times to create an extremely smooth sauce, which adds to the delicate texture of the fish.

Pescado con Caldo de Ancho y Chorizo

SEARED WHITEFISH WITH ANCHO-CHORIZO BROTH

The ancho chile pepper is widely used in Mexican cooking and has a mild heat combined with a sweet, fruity flavor, which makes it perfect for seasoning fish.

In this recipe, whitefish is lightly sautéed, combined with clams and shrimp and then topped with a rich sauce of ancho chile pepper and tomatoes. The deep flavors of this dish are further intensified with the addition of spicy Mexican chorizo.

Finishing the cooking process of the fish in the sauce ensures that it is cooked through but doesn't dry out. You can even make the sauce in advance and finish it later with the addition of the seafood, making it the perfect meal for a quick dinner or entertaining.

Serve with warm tortillas or toasted bread and a nice glass of Spanish Albariño.

YIELD: 4 SERVINGS

ANCHO-CHORIZO BROTH

1 tbsp (15 ml) canola oil

1 cup (227 g) Mexican chorizo (page 14)

2 shallots, diced

4 garlic cloves, minced

1 pt (322 g) cherry tomatoes, halved

3 cups (700 ml) chicken broth

1 cup (240 ml) dry white wine

1 pinch ancho chile powder

1 tsp salt

4 (6 oz [170 g]) whitefish filets (I recommend halibut or cod)

Salt and pepper

¼ cup (59 ml) olive oil

8 large shrimp, peeled and deveined

8 littleneck clams, scrubbed

2 tbsp (5 g) cilantro leaves, chopped

1 lime

ANCHO-CHORIZO BROTH

Heat the canola oil in a large sauté pan over medium-high heat until the oil begins to shimmer. Stir in the chorizo and cook for approximately 8 minutes, stirring often, until the fat renders and the chorizo begins to brown. Using a slotted spoon, remove the chorizo from the pan and place on a paper towel-lined plate to drain. Drain all but 1 tablespoon (15 ml) of the oil from the pan.

Return the pan to the heat, add the shallots and cook for 3 minutes, until they begin to soften. Add the garlic and tomatoes and continue to cook for 2 minutes. Stir in the broth, white wine, ancho powder and salt and bring to a simmer.

Meanwhile, pat the whitefish fillets dry with a clean paper towel and season with salt and pepper. Heat 2 tablespoons (30 ml) of the olive oil in a large sauté pan over medium-high heat until shimmering. Place the fish into the pan, skin side down, and cook for 4 minutes, until nicely browned on the bottom. Using a fish spatula, gently move the fish from the sauté pan and place, skin side up, in the pan with the Ancho-Chorizo Broth. Reduce the heat to medium-low and nestle the shrimp and the clams around the fish.

Cover the pan and simmer for 8-10 minutes, or until the clams have opened. Remove the pan from the heat and discard any unopened clams. Sprinkle with cilantro and drizzle with a squeeze of lime. Taste and add additional salt if desired.

Arroz a la Tumbada

VERACRUZ-STYLE SEAFOOD RICE

Arroz a la Tumbada is a traditional dish originating in Veracruz, Mexico, that combines all of the briny flavors of the sea. It's an impressive dish with lots of Mexican flair. The texture should be slightly soupier than the Spanish paella, but with a slight kick from the chile peppers. If you are a fan of seafood and rice, you will absolutely love this dish.

Feel free to use the seafood listed below or a combination of your favorites to create a truly unique dish.

YIELD: 6 SERVINGS

1½ cups (320 g) long-grain white rice

6 Roma tomatoes

6 Roma tomatoes, quartered

3 tbsp (45 ml) olive oil, plus more for drizzling

1 large white onion, diced

3 garlic cloves, minced

4 cups (950 ml) fish or chicken broth

3 fresh jalapeño chiles, thinly sliced

1 tsp salt

12 large prawns, heads and tails in tact

12 clams, scrubbed

6 soft-shell crabs, cut in half, or ½ lb (227 g) frozen crab claws

Place the rice in a large bowl and cover with warm water; let sit for 5 minutes. Drain through a colander and rinse under cold water for 2–3 minutes, or until the water runs clear. Shake the colander to remove any excess water and let sit in the sink for 3–4 minutes to continue draining.

Place the 6 whole Roma tomatoes in a blender and puree until smooth. Once pureed, pour the tomato mixture into a bowl and incorporate the remaining 6 quartered tomatoes.

Heat 1 tablespoon (15 ml) of the olive oil in a medium-size saucepan over medium heat until the oil begins to shimmer. Stir in the diced onion and 3 cloves of the minced garlic and cook for approximately 8–10 minutes, or until the onions are translucent and the garlic begins to turn a golden brown. Add the tomato mixture, bring to a simmer and cook for an additional 5 minutes, until the oil begins to appear on the surface.

Meanwhile, heat the remaining 2 tablespoons (30 ml) olive oil in a large saucepan or Dutch oven until hot and shimmering. Add the rice cook over medium heat, stirring often, for approximately 3–5 minutes, until the rice begins to brown slightly. Stir in the tomato mixture, broth, jalapeños and salt. Taste and season with additional salt if necessary. Turn the heat down to low, cover and cook for approximately 15 minutes, until the rice is slightly al dente. The mixture should be very soupy.

Add the prawns, clams and crab to the pan. Cover and cook an additional 5 minutes, or until the clams are open and the crab and shrimp are cooked through and begin to turn a reddish color. Discard any unopened clams. Drizzle with olive oil and serve immediately.

Pescado Zarandeado

RED CHILE–GRILLED WHOLE FISH

This dish originated in the state of Nayarit on Mexico's Pacific coast. The flavor is very complex, combining the earthy piquancy of the guajillo peppers with the crisp skin and moist, sweet meat of the fish.

Grilling a whole fish might seem intimidating, but it is actually quite simple and creates a truly dramatic presentation. The Tomato-Serrano Sauce adds an extra flavor component and further enhances the taste and show-stopping presentation of the dish.

YIELD: 6 SERVINGS

1 (3–4 lb [1.4–1.8 kg]) whole fish (I recommend branzino or red snapper)

8 dried guajillo chile peppers, stemmed and seeded

½ cup (118 ml) soy sauce

¼ cup (59 ml) lime juice

2 serrano chile peppers

1 tbsp (1.6 g) dried oregano, preferably Mexican

2 garlic cloves

1 tsp ground black pepper

1 tsp salt

TOMATO-SERRANO SAUCE

8 Roma tomatoes

4 garlic cloves

2 serrano chile peppers

Salt

Cilantro springs, for garnish

Lime wedges, for garnish

Tortillas, for serving

Preheat a grill or grill pan to medium heat. If you are using a charcoal grill, light the fire and let the coals burn until covered with gray ash. Clean the grates and brush with a light coating of olive oil to prevent the fish from sticking.

Clean and scale the fish, or have your fishmonger do it for you. Using a sharp knife, gently score the fish by making deep, angled cuts to the bone at every 1½ inches (3.8 cm).

Heat a medium cast-iron skillet or heavy-bottomed sauté pan over medium-high heat. Once the pan is hot, cook the guajillo chiles for approximately 30 seconds per side, or until slightly toasty. Be careful not to over-toast the chiles and allow them to turn black, as this will make the sauce bitter. Remove the toasted chiles from the pan and place in a bowl. Cover and submerge completely with hot water and set aside for 15 minutes to rehydrate.

Using a slotted spoon, remove the chiles from the water and place in a blender. Discard the soaking liquid. Add the soy sauce, lime juice, serrano chile peppers, oregano, garlic and black pepper to the blender and puree into a smooth paste.

Season the entire fish, including the cavity, with the salt. Place the fish in a shallow baking dish and pour the marinade on top. Let stand for 30 minutes.

Remove the fish from the marinade and grill directly over a low fire or heat. Resist the urge to move the fish around or you could run the risk of ripping the skin and lose flesh. Wait 3–4 minutes until the skin no longer sticks to the grill, slide an oiled spatula gently under the fish and gradually turn over and cook for an additional 3–4 minutes until the skin is crisp and the flesh is moist and flaky.

TOMATO-SERRANO SAUCE

Meanwhile, prepare the sauce by placing the tomatoes, unpeeled garlic and serrano chile pepper on the grill. Grill for 3–4 minutes, or until lightly blackened. Remove from the heat and peel the garlic and tomatoes, discarding the skins. Place the peeled garlic, tomatoes and serrano chile pepper in a blender or food processer and blend to a puree. Season to taste with salt.

To serve, transfer the fish to a large platter. Garnish with a sprig of cilantro and serve alongside the tomato sauce with lime wedges and tortillas.

Note: I've made this recipe using a whole fish but feel free to use fish fillets instead.

In Mexico, Pescado Zarandeado is often cooked directly over mangrove wood, which further adds to its intense flavor. You can also grill the fish over mesquite wood, creating an amazing element to this already fantastic dish.

Pescado Veracruzano

VERACRUZ-STYLE FISH

The ingredients in Pescado Veracruzano may seem like ones from a dish originated in the Mediterranean, but in fact it's a regional specialty of the Veracruz state of Mexico and yet another delicious example of how Mexican cuisine has been influenced by European settlers.

The dish is bursting with rich color and fresh, straightforward, clean flavor. The fish is first marinated in lime juice and then added to a sauce of tomatoes, garlic, spices, olives and briny capers. The final topping of Jalapeños en Escabeche adds a nice touch of acidity and heat to the dish.

At the restaurants, we top the completed dish with grilled slices of fresh tomato to add a nice charred, sweet flavor, but you can omit this extra step if you are short on time.

YIELD: 4 SERVINGS

4 (6 oz [170 g]) whitefish fillets (I prefer cod or halibut)

2 tsp (10 g) salt

½ cup (120 ml) lime juice, preferably freshly squeezed

¼ cup (60 ml) olive oil

1 small white onion, thinly sliced

4 garlic cloves, minced

6 Roma tomatoes, diced

2 cups (360 g) green manzanilla olives, halved

2 tbsp (22.5 g) Spanish capers

2 tbsp (19 g) black raisins

2 bay leaves

2 sprigs fresh thyme

2 sprigs fresh oregano

¼ cup (45 g) Jalapeños en Escabeche (page 123) or store-bought

¼ cup (10 g) cilantro leaves, chopped

OPTIONAL, FOR GARNISH
2 heirloom or beefy tomatoes, sliced

Lightly pat the fish fillets dry with a clean paper towel and evenly season with 1 teaspoon of the salt. Place the fillets in a glass baking dish and top with the lime juice. Refrigerate for 30 minutes to 1 hour.

Meanwhile, heat the olive oil in a large cast-iron skillet or Dutch oven over medium-high heat until the oil is very hot and begins to shimmer. Stir in the onion and cook for 3–5 minutes, or until the onion begins to soften. Add the garlic and continue to cook for another minute. Stir in the tomatoes and cook the mixture for an additional 10 minutes, until the tomatoes begin to soften and release their juices.

Reduce the heat to medium-low and add the olives, capers, raisins, bay leaves, thyme, oregano and pickled jalapeños to the pan. Season with the remaining 1 teaspoon salt and cook for an additional 15 minutes.

Remove the fish from the marinade and gently nestle on top of the sauce. Cover the pan with a tight-fitting lid or double layer of aluminum foil and cook for 4 minutes. Gently turn the fish over and cook for an additional 4 minutes, or until the fish is opaque and begins to flake.

Remove the bay leaves, oregano and thyme sprigs. Sprinkle with chopped cilantro, taste and season with additional salt (if desired) and serve. Garnish with slices of grilled tomatoes (optional).

Mejillones con Tequila

SAUTÉED MEXICAN MUSSELS WITH CHORIZO AND TEQUILA

When I first began developing a recipe for Mexican mussels, I spoke with my restaurant partner, Sergio Ramos, who was born and raised in Mexico. I asked him about the way he would eat mussels growing up; his response: "We would simply pick them up off of the beach and eat them raw."

While I appreciate that approach, I don't recommend it. I have since developed a rustic recipe full of traditional Mexican flavors. White wine, garlic, jalapeños and tomato help create a garlicky, fragrant flavor, while chorizo adds to the spice and provides an extra touch of traditional Mexican taste. A drizzle of tequila perks up the flavors even further.

Serve with warm tortillas or grilled crusty bread, as you won't want to waste one single drop of the rich broth.

YIELD: 2 LARGE OR 4 SMALL SERVINGS

---

3 tbsp (45 ml) olive oil

8 oz (227 g) Mexican chorizo (fresh, page 15, or store-bought), casings removed

1 tbsp (15 g) minced shallot

3 garlic cloves, thinly sliced

2 tsp (3.5 g) finely chopped fresh jalapeño pepper

1½ cups (360 ml) dry white wine

4 Roma tomatoes, diced

2 lb (907 g) mussels, scrubbed and de-bearded

1 tsp salt

⅓ cup (13 g) fresh cilantro leaves, coarsely chopped

½ cup (120 ml) good-quality silver tequila, (I recommend Herradura Silver)

Bread or tortillas, for serving

Heat the olive oil in a heavy-bottomed sauté pan over medium-high heat. Once the oil is shimmering, but not smoking, add the chorizo and cook for approximately 8 minutes, stirring often, until the sausage is thoroughly cooked through. Remove the chorizo from the pan and pat dry with a paper towel to remove any excess oil. Discard all but approximately 1 tablespoon (15 ml) of the chorizo fat from the pan.

Add the minced shallot to the pan with the chorizo oil and cook for about 3 minutes, stirring occasionally, until soft. Add the sliced garlic and diced jalapeño and cook an additional 3 minutes, stirring occasionally, until both are cooked through.

Keep the pan on medium-high heat and return the chorizo to the pan. Stir in the wine, tomatoes and then the mussels. Sprinkle the salt over the mixture and bring to a boil.

Once the mixture has reached a boil, cover the pan with aluminum foil or a heavy lid and cook for approximately 8 minutes, or until the majority of the mussels have opened.

Remove from the heat and discard any unopened mussels. Spoon the mussels and broth into serving bowls, sprinkle with chopped cilantro and top with a drizzle of tequila. Serve with crusty bread or fresh corn tortillas.

Caldo de Mariscos

MEXICAN SEAFOOD STEW

In this luscious seafood stew, a mixture of squid, mussels, shrimp and whitefish are combined in a rich broth of earthy guajillo chiles and sweet, roasted tomatoes. I've listed my favorite combination of seafood, but feel free to use any seafood you like, as there are no real rules to this recipe except to use what is fresh. You can also cut down on cooking time by not making your own fish stock, and use a good-quality store-bought fish stock in its place. The resulting flavor will still be excellent although slightly different.

YIELD: 6 SERVINGS

FISH STOCK
2 tbsp (30 ml) olive oil

1 shallot, diced

1 fresh jalapeño pepper, diced

1 large carrot, cut into ¼" (6 mm)-thick coins

1 celery stalk, sliced

6 garlic cloves, diced

6 sprigs fresh thyme

3 dried bay leaves

8 black peppercorns

3 lb (1.4 kg) rinsed fish bones or shrimp (or a combination of both)

1 cup (240 ml) dry white wine

8 cups (2 L) water

RED CHILE PASTE
8 dried guajillo chile peppers, stems, seeds and ribs removed

½ medium white onion, dry roasted (page 18)

4 garlic cloves, dry roasted and peeled (page 18)

4 Roma tomatoes, dry roasted (page 18)

6 cup (1440 ml) prepared fish stock (recipe above) or water

4 tsp (20 g) salt

SEAFOOD
1 lb (454 g) mussels or clams, cleaned

1 lb (454 g) lean whitefish filets (I recommend cod, rock fish or halibut), cut into 1" (2.5 cm) chunks

1 lb (454 g) large shrimp, peeled and deveined

1 lb (454 g) squid, cut into ¼" (6 mm)-thick rings

OPTIONAL, FOR GARNISH
½ cup (20 g) cilantro leaves, chopped

2 limes, cut into wedges

Crusty bread

FISH STOCK
In a very large stockpot, heat the olive oil until hot, but not smoking. Add the shallot, jalapeño, carrot, celery and garlic and cook over medium-high heat for about 3–4 minutes, until the garlic is cooked through and just golden. Stir in the fresh thyme, bay leaves and peppercorns. Add the fish bones, white wine and water, and bring to a boil. Once the mixture begins to boil, immediately reduce the heat to medium–low and simmer, uncovered, for 30 minutes.

After 30 minutes, remove from the heat and strain through a medium-mesh strainer or colander. Set the fish stock aside and discard the fish bones and solids.

RED CHILE PASTE
Heat a medium-size cast-iron skillet or heavy-bottomed sauté pan over medium-high heat. Once the pan is hot, cook the chile peppers for approximately 30 seconds per side, until slightly toasty. Be careful not to over-toast the chiles and allow them to turn black, as this will make the stew bitter. Remove from the pan and place in a bowl, cover completely with hot water and set aside for 15 minutes to rehydrate.

After 15 minutes, remove the rehydrated chiles from the water with a slotted spoon and place in a blender. Discard the soaking liquid. Add the onion, garlic, tomatoes and 1 cup (237 ml) of the fish stock to the blender and puree into a thick sauce. Season with the salt and combine with the remaining 5 cups (1.2 L) fish stock.

SEAFOOD
Simmer the red chile fish stock mixture in a very large stockpot over medium heat for 15 minutes. Stir the mussels into the broth, cover and simmer for 3 minutes, until the mussels just begin to open. Stir in the whitefish, shrimp and squid and cook, covered, for an additional 4–5 minutes, until the shrimp is cooked through and the tails begin to curl into a "C" shape.

Remove the stew from the heat and discard any unopened mussels. Spoon the stew into individual bowls and top with chopped cilantro and a squeeze of lime. Serve with a plate of crusty, grilled bread.

Taco de Langosta de Puerto Nuevo

PUERTO NUEVO LOBSTER TACO

In the fishing village of Puerto Nuevo in the Baja region of Mexico they serve the most amazing pan-fried lobster tacos. Inspired by the delicious tacos from that small fishing village, I've created a decadent version using sweet Maine lobster, my favorite tequila and rich duck fat in place of the typical pork lard. If you don't have access to duck fat, use butter or bacon drippings.

Chipotle pepper adds to the bold flavor and creates a nice heat level in the dish. Don't forget the final squeeze of lime at the end as it balances the dish with a touch of acidity.

I drank a classic margarita while I tasted my first lobster taco in Mexico and this dish pairs equally well with my Classic Zapoteca Margarita (page 175).

YIELD: 4 SERVINGS

---

4 tbsp (60 g) salt

2 (12 oz [340 ml]) cans dark Mexican beer

2 (1–1.5 lb [454–680 g]) live lobsters

2 tbsp (30 ml) duck fat or good-quality lard

2 tsp (5 g) chipotle powder

1 tsp salt

¼ cup (60 ml) silver tequila (I recomend Herradura Silver)

2 tbsp (5 g) cilantro leaves, chopped

1 lime, cut into wedges

Fresh or store-bought corn tortillas

1 avocado, peeled, pitted and sliced

1 cup (226 g) Salsa Mexicana (page 158)

Fill a large stockpot half full of water, stir in the salt and 2 cans of dark Mexican beer and bring to a boil over medium-high heat. When the water has come to a rolling boil, plunge the lobsters into the pot, head first. Cover with a tight-fitting lid and bring back to a boil. Reduce the heat to medium-low and simmer for 6 minutes, until just cooked through and the shells turn bright red. Lift the lobsters out of the water with tongs and place in a colander to drain and cool slightly.

Place each lobster, belly side up, on a cutting board with the tail facing you. Beginning at the point where the tail meets the body, cut the tail in half lengthwise. Rotate the lobster so that the head is closest to you and repeat the process, cutting through the body and head. With a knife, remove the claws from the body. Using the back of the knife, tap the claws until the shells crack.

Separate the halves and gently rinse under cold water to remove the black digestive tract from the tail and head sack from the head. Repeat the process with the remaining lobster. Set aside.

Heat the duck fat or lard in a large sauté pan over medium-high heat until hot. Place the lobster halves in the pan, shell side down, along with the claws. Sprinkle each lobster half with ½ teaspoon of chipotle powder and ¼ teaspoon of salt and cook for 3 minutes. Turn the lobsters over and cook the other side for an additional 2 minutes. Remove the pan from the heat add the tequila to the pan. Be careful, as the pan will ignite. Cook until the flames die down.

Remove the lobster pieces from the pan and place on a serving platter. Spoon the tequila sauce on top of the lobster meat. Sprinkle with chopped cilantro and a squeeze of lime. Serve with warm tortillas, avocado slices and Salsa Mexicana to make your own taco.

Note: Lobster should be purchased alive and kept alive until you're ready to cook them.

five

Sopas, Ensaladas y Guarniciones

SOUPS, SALADS AND SIDES

Whether at home or at the restaurants, I love to make soup. At home, the smell of soup simmering on the stove is something I look forward to, especially when the temperature starts to drop.

Like soup, many of the side dishes in this chapter, can be made days in advance and refrigerated until you're ready to enjoy them. Many things like the Pickled Red Onions and Yucatán Jalapeños en Escabeche can even be canned so that you can simply open a jar and enjoy them at a moment's notice.

Unfortunately, the salads are not as forgiving and need to be dressed just prior to serving. The dressing, however, can be made in advance to make things simpler and perfect for a quick weeknight meal.

Sopa de Calabaza

ROASTED OAXACAN-SPICED ORANGE AND BUTTERNUT SQUASH SOUP

I often serve a version of this soup at many of my restaurants' chef's tasting dinners, and have even prepared it for a dinner at the James Beard House.

The long list of ingredients might seem daunting, but once all of the components are organized, the soup is quite easy to complete and the flavors are absolutely amazing.

You can skip the optional grated chocolate garnish, but I highly recommend you try it at least once. The combination of the sweet chocolate with the savory components of the dish is surprisingly delicious, and has even been referred to by one restaurant critic as "insanely wonderful."

YIELD: 6 SERVINGS

---

2 lb (907 g) butternut squash, peeled, cleaned and diced into 2" (5 cm) pieces

2 medium white onions, peeled and quartered

5 garlic cloves

½ tsp ground cinnamon

1 orange, halved

¼ cup (50 g) light brown sugar

2 tbsp (30 ml) olive oil

½ cup (120 ml) orange juice

3 whole allspice berries

5 whole black peppercorns

2 tsp (10 g) salt

3 fresh thyme sprigs

2 poblano chile peppers, dry roasted, stemmed, seeded and peeled (page 18)

4 cups (950 ml) vegetable or chicken broth

2 cups (480 ml) heavy cream

¼ tsp ground nutmeg, plus more for garnish

Chocolate, grated (preferably good-quality Mexican chocolate)

Preheat the oven to 400°F (204°C).

In a large roasting pan, combine the diced squash, onions, garlic, cinnamon, orange halves, brown sugar, olive oil, orange juice, allspice berries, peppercorns and salt. Toss to thoroughly combine. Top with the fresh thyme sprigs and cover tightly with two layers of aluminum foil. Place in the preheated oven and roast for 1 hour, until the squash is fork-tender.

Remove the pan from the oven and discard the orange halves and thyme sprigs. Puree the roasted mixture in a blender (or with an immersion blender) along with the poblano chile peppers and broth. Blend until extremely smooth.

Add the puree to a large stockpot. Stir in the heavy cream and nutmeg. Taste and season with additional salt, if necessary. Simmer over medium heat for 30 minutes, until all flavors are thoroughly combined.

Ladle into soup bowls and top with the grated chocolate and additional nutmeg if desired.

Sopa Langosta con Maiz y Chile Poblano

CORN, POBLANO AND LOBSTER BISQUE

I was asked to prepare a dish for the Mexican Consulate that contained the traditional flavors of Mexican cuisine combined with the amazing, local products abundant in New England. I created this version of New England lobster bisque utilizing succulent Maine lobster, sweet corn (which is an essential part of Mexican culture) and the versatile, slightly spicy poblano chile.

The additional depth of flavor comes from using the lobster shells in the stock, as well as including the corncobs. The natural sweetness of both the lobster and the corn is complemented by the charred, smoky flavor of the fire-roasted poblano chile peppers. These flavors combine to create a rich, decadent soup with a hint of spice.

YIELD: 6 SERVINGS

2 ears corn

4 tbsp (68 g) salt

2 (12 oz [340 ml]) cans dark Mexican beer

4 (2 lb [907 g]) lobsters

2 tbsp (29 g) unsalted butter

4 cups (606 g) diced white onion

2 cups (480 ml) dry white wine

6 cups (1.4 L) water

6 garlic cloves, dry roasted, peeled and finely chopped (page 18)

3 poblano chile peppers, dry roasted, stemmed, seeded and peeled (page 18)

3 cups (710 ml) heavy cream

½ tsp white pepper

1 tbsp (2.5 g) cilantro leaves, chopped, for garnish (optional)

Remove and discard the husks and silk from the ears of corn. Arrange the corn on a tray in a single layer and broil for 15 minutes, turning every 5 minutes, until slightly charred and blackened. Remove from the broiler and cut away the corn kernels, reserving the cobs to use for the stock.

Fill a large stockpot half full with water. Stir in the salt and the beer, and bring to a boil over medium-high heat. Once boiling, plunge the lobsters into the pot, head first. Cover with a tight-fitting lid and bring back to a boil.

Reduce the heat to medium-low and simmer for 10–12 minutes, until cooked through and the shells turn bright red. Lift the lobsters out of the water with tongs and place in a colander to drain and cool slightly.

Once cool enough to handle, shuck the lobsters and remove and roughly chop the meat. Reserve the shells for the stock and shucked claws for garnish.

Heat 1 tablespoon (15 g) of the butter in a medium-size stockpot over medium-high heat. Stir 1 cup (151 g) of the diced onions into the pan and sauté for 5 minutes until just soft. Add the lobster shells, reserved corncobs and 1 cup (240 ml) of the white wine to the pot. Bring the mixture to a boil.

Add the water to the pot and simmer, uncovered, for 15-20 minutes over medium-high heat, until the stock is reduced to approximately 5 cups (1.2 L). Remove from the heat and strain through a fine-mesh strainer. Set the stock aside and discard the lobster shells, corncobs and any other large bits.

Heat the remaining 1 tablespoon (15 g) butter in a medium-size stockpot over medium-high heat. Stir the remaining 3 cups (455 g) onions into the pan and sauté for 5 minutes until just soft. Add the garlic and cook for an additional 2 minutes, until golden brown. Add the remaining 1 cup (240 ml) white wine and reduce for 1 minute. Add the broiled corn kernels and 5 cups (1.2 L) of the reserved broth to the pan and simmer, uncovered, for 15 minutes.

Remove the mixture from the heat and let cool slightly. Transfer to a blender along with the peeled poblano chile peppers and puree (in multiple batches if necessary) until extremely smooth. Strain the mixture through a fine-mesh strainer, pressing hard to extract as much as possible. Discard of any large particles (there should be less than ¼ cup [60 ml] of large particles left in the strainer). Place the mixture in a clean stockpot and bring to a simmer over medium heat.

Meanwhile, heat the heavy cream in separate saucepan over low heat and reduce for 10 minutes. Add the reduced heavy cream to the stock. Stir in the chopped lobster tail and leg meat, reserving the claws for garnish. Season to taste with salt and white pepper. Ladle the bisque into soup bowls and garnish with the reserved lobster claws and chopped cilantro, if desired.

Sopa Azteca

CHICKEN TORTILLA SOUP

Often called tortilla soup, Sopa Azteca is found throughout Mexico and is the ultimate comfort food. There are many variations, but this one includes rich, fruity ancho chile peppers.

Simmering the chicken in water, onions and garlic not only keeps the meat moist, but also provides a flavorful broth to use as a base for the soup. The addition of fire-roasted tomatoes and piquant ancho chile peppers lends a nice fiery, slightly spicy depth of flavor.

When serving, the chicken and other garnishes are arranged in the center of a bowl before pouring the piping hot stock around them. This creates a nice visual impact to the dish and helps bring the chicken back up to temperature.

YIELD: 6 SERVINGS

SOUP

½ cup (20 g) fresh cilantro stems, chopped

2 tbsp (30 g) salt

1 tsp black peppercorns

2 garlic cloves

1 white onion, quartered

1 bay leaf

16 cups (3.8 L) water

4 boneless, skinless chicken breasts, rinsed

2 tbsp (30 ml) canola oil

1 white onion, julienned

4 garlic cloves, chopped

2 dried ancho chile peppers, stemmed, seeded, dry roasted and rehydrated (page 18)

6 Roma tomatoes, dry roasted (page 18)

1 corn tortilla, torn into 2" (5 cm) pieces

2 sprigs fresh oregano

TORTILLA STRIPS

½ cup (120 ml) canola oil

4 tortillas, cut into ¼" (6 mm)-thick strips

GARNISH

2 avocados, peeled, pitted and sliced

1 cup (130 g) queso fresco or shredded Monterey Jack cheese

2 tbsp (5 g) cilantro leaves, chopped

1 lime, cut into wedges

SOUP

Place the cilantro, salt, peppercorns, whole garlic cloves, quartered onion and bay leaf in a heavy large stockpot and cover completely with the water; bring to a boil over medium-high heat. Add the chicken breasts. Simmer, uncovered, for 20 minutes, until cooked through and tender. Remove from the heat and set aside to cool.

Strain the mixture through a colander, reserving the cooking liquid to use in the soup. Discard the onion, garlic and bay leaf.

Place the chicken on a cutting board and roughly shred. Set aside.

Heat 1 tablespoon (15 ml) of the canola oil in a medium-size stockpot over medium-high heat. Sauté the juilienned onion for 5 minutes, until just soft. Add the chopped garlic and cook for an additional 2 minutes, until golden brown. Using a slotted spoon, remove the onions and garlic from the pan and place in a blender along with the rehydrated chile peppers, tomatoes and tortilla. Puree for 2 minutes until extremely smooth.

Return the stockpot to the heat and heat the remaining 1 tablespoon (15 ml) of canola oil until shimmering. Add the puree, stir and cook for 5 minutes, until it thickens and darkens slightly.

Reduce the heat to medium-low and stir 8 cups (1.9 L) of the reserved chicken cooking liquid into the pureed mixture, along with the fresh oregano. Simmer the mixture, uncovered, for 10 minutes. Remove the oregano sprigs from the soup and season to taste with salt and pepper.

TORTILLA STRIPS

Heat the canola oil in a sauté pan over medium-high heat until shimmering. Gently place the tortilla strips into the oil and immediately stir. Fry the tortillas for approximately 2 minutes, until golden brown. Remove with a slotted spoon and place on a paper towel to drain.

To serve, place a large spoonful of shredded chicken in the middle of a large bowl and ladle the tortilla soup around the chicken. Garnish with a slice of avocado, some queso fresco, chopped cilantro, a squeeze of lime juice and some of the tortilla strips.

Note: For a more complex taste, sprinkle crumbled, crisp ancho chiles on top of your soup just prior to serving.

Sopa de Chile Poblano

ROASTED POBLANO SOUP

Fire-roasted poblano chile peppers add a rich, smoky depth of flavor and distinctive green color to this dish. It is a deliciously creamy soup that also highlights sweet summer corn.

YIELD: 6 SERVINGS

2 tbsp (29 g) unsalted butter

1 large white onion, roughly chopped

2 garlic cloves, finely diced

1 celery stalk, roughly chopped

1 medium carrot, roughly chopped

2 cups (303 g) fresh corn, removed from the cob

8 fresh poblano chiles, fire roasted, peeled, stemmed, seeded and roughly chopped (page 18)

4 cups (950 ml) chicken or vegetable broth

2 cups (473 ml) whole milk

1 cup (237 ml) heavy cream

Salt

¼ cup (10 g) fresh cilantro leaves, finely chopped

Heat the butter in a medium-size saucepan over medium-high heat until the butter is very hot, but not smoking. Add the diced onions, garlic, celery and carrot to the pan and cook for approximately 10 minutes until soft, stirring occasionally. Add the corn kernels and chopped poblanos and cook for an additional 3 minutes.

Stir in the stock and milk and bring to a simmer. Reduce the heat to medium-low and simmer for an additional 30 minutes, stirring occasionally, until the mixture is slightly reduced.

Remove the soup from the heat and stir in the heavy cream. Using an immersion or stand blender, puree for 1–2 minutes, until extremely smooth.

Season to taste with salt. Serve the soup very hot garnished with fresh cilantro leaves.

Note: I prefer this soup pureed until it is perfectly smooth, but you can puree it less (or not at all) if you prefer more texture.

Ensalada Cesar Mexicana

GRILLED MEXICAN CAESAR SALAD WITH POBLANO–PUMPKIN SEED DRESSING

Poblano chile peppers and pumpkin seeds are essential ingredients in Mexican cuisine. In this dish, they are combined to create a bold, creamy dressing. The charred, crisp edges of the grilled romaine lettuce adds a slight smoky flavor and contrasts perfectly with the silky texture of the pumpkin seed dressing. The chile-spiced grilled bread finishes the dish with additional texture and a hint of spice. For a heartier salad, top with grilled chicken or shrimp.

YIELD: 6 SERVINGS

POBLANO-PUMPKIN SEED DRESSING
1 poblano chile pepper, fire roasted, peeled, stemmed and seeded (page 18)

½ cup (63 g) pumpkin seeds, dry roasted (page 18)

2 garlic cloves, dry roasted and peeled (page 18)

¾ cup (177 ml) olive oil

2 tbsp (30 ml) red wine vinegar

3 tbsp (23 g) Mexican cotija or Romano cheese

1½ cups (6 g) cilantro leaves, chopped

4 tbsp (60 ml) water

¾ cup (90 g) Mexican crema (page 15)

1 tbsp (15 ml) lime juice

½ tsp salt

CHILE-SPICED GRILLED BREAD
4 tbsp (57 g) unsalted butter

2 garlic cloves, minced

¼ tsp salt

12 slices crusty bread, cut into ¼" (6 mm)-thick slices

¼ tsp chile de árbol powder

SALAD
3 hearts romaine lettuce

Salt

½ cup (60 g) Mexican cotija cheese

OPTIONAL, FOR GARNISH
¼ cup (31 g) pumpkin seeds

POBLANO-PUMPKIN SEED DRESSING
Place all of the ingredients for the dressing in a blender or food processor and blend to a smooth puree. Taste and season with additional salt if desired. Set aside.

CHILE-SPICED GRILLED BREAD
Preheat a grill or grill pan to medium heat. If you are using a charcoal grill, light the fire and let the coals burn until they are covered with gray ash. Clean the grates and brush with a light coating of olive oil.

Place the butter in a small saucepan and melt over medium heat. Add the garlic to the pan and raise the heat to medium. Cook for 2–3 minutes, until the garlic is fragrant and begins to brown. Season with salt and lightly brush the butter onto the sliced bread. Place the slices directly on the grill and cook for 1–2 minutes per side, until lightly charred. Remove from heat and lightly dust with the chile de árbol powder and set aside.

SALAD
Cut the romaine hearts in half, lengthwise, and place on the grill, cut side down. Cook for approximately 2 minutes, until grill marks begin to appear. Turn the lettuce halves over and grill the other side for an additional minute. Remove the romaine from the heat and cut off the base stems. Gently spread the leaves across a plate or serving platter.

Drizzle the salad with the Poblano–Pumpkin Seed Dressing and sprinkle lightly with the salt, cotija cheese and pumpkin seeds, if desired. Serve warm with a side of the chile-spiced grilled bread.

Note: Caesar salad may not seem Mexican to most people, but it was actually invented in the Mexican city of Tijuana by Caesar Cardini in 1924.

Ensalada de Aguacate

GOLDEN AVOCADO SALAD WITH JALAPEÑO-CILANTRO VINAIGRETTE

Avocados are amazing by themselves, but by lightly breading and frying them, they take on a whole new flavor. Fried avocados are absolutely creamy and luscious on the inside and crisp and flaky on the outside. They have the perfect textural contrast.

The bold Jalapeño-Cilantro Vinaigrette brightens the flavors of this salad while the crisp arugula complements the entire dish with a nice peppery flavor.

YIELD: 4 SERVINGS

JALAPEÑO-CILANTRO VINAIGRETTE

1 cup (40 g) cilantro leaves

2 small jalapeño peppers, stems removed

½ cup (120 ml) white wine vinegar

Juice of 2 limes

1 garlic clove

½ tsp salt

1 cup (240 ml) extra virgin olive oil

FRIED AVOCADO

½ cup (63 g) all-purpose flour

2 eggs, slightly beaten

1 cup (60 g) panko breadcrumbs

2 avocados, peeled, pitted and cut into 1" (2.5 cm) wedges, 6 wedges per avocado

Salt

2 cups (480 ml) canola oil

SALAD

12 cups (240 g) baby arugula

Salt

Freshly ground black pepper

1 pt (320 g) cherry tomatoes, halved

JALAPEÑO-CILANTRO VINAIGRETTE

In a blender, puree the cilantro, jalapeños, vinegar, lime juice, garlic and salt until smooth. Slowly drizzle in the olive oil until thoroughly combined. Set aside.

FRIED AVOCADO

Place the flour, eggs and panko into 3 separate, shallow bowls. Season the avocado with salt and dredge in the flour (shaking off any excess), beaten egg and then panko. Place on a parchment-lined tray and repeat with the remaining avocado wedges.

Heat the canola oil in a Dutch oven over medium-high heat until shimmering. Gently place the breaded avocado wedges (in batches if necessary) into the oil and cook for approximately 3 minutes, turning once, until they are golden brown. Transfer to a paper-lined tray to drain.

SALAD

Place the arugula in a large bowl and toss with the Jalapeño-Cilantro Vinaigrette. Season with salt and freshly ground pepper. Divide the arugula among 4 dinner plates, sprinkle with the cherry tomatoes and top with the golden avocado.

Note: Fried avocados are simply fantastic on this salad but they also taste great eaten by themselves topped with a little Salsa Mexicana (page 158).

Ensalada de Nopales

GRILLED CACTUS PADDLE SALAD

Nopales, or the paddles of the prickly pear cactus, are a staple in the Mexican diet. They have a flavor that is often described as similar to green beans or okra. This dish makes a distinctive main course, topped with fresh avocado, or as a side dish served alongside grilled beef or chicken.

YIELD: 6 SERVINGS

DRESSING
½ cup (120 ml) apple cider vinegar

1 tbsp (3 g) fresh oregano

1 tbsp (5 g) red pepper flakes

½ tsp salt

½ cup (120 ml) olive oil

SALAD
6 nopales, thorns removed

Olive oil

Salt and pepper

2 radishes, thinly sliced

¼ cup (10 g) cilantro leaves, chopped

DRESSING
Combine the apple cider vinegar, oregano, red pepper flakes and salt in a medium-size bowl. Slowly drizzle in the olive oil and whisk to thoroughly combine.

SALAD
With a paring knife, trim any remaining thorns from the nopales. Trim ¼ inch (6 mm) of the outside edges, leaving the base attached. Cut the top of the nopales into ⅓-inch (8.5 mm)-thick strips, being careful to only cut to the edge of the base so that the strips are still attached. Lightly brush the nopales strips with olive oil and season with salt and pepper.

Preheat an outdoor grill or grill pan to medium-high heat. Brush the grill grates lightly with olive oil to prevent the nopales from sticking. Lay the paddles directly on the grill and cook for approximately 5 minutes per side, until slightly charred. Remove from the grill and cut into 1-inch (2.5 cm) pieces, discarding the base.

Combine the grilled nopales strips with the radishes and chopped cilantro and toss with the vinaigrette. Taste and season with additional salt if desired.

Note: The freshest cactus paddles are bright green and firm. Look for them in the produce section of you gourmet grocery or Latin market.

Rajas con Crema

ROASTED POBLANOS WITH CREAM

Rajas literally means "slices" in Spanish, and that is exactly what this dish is: tender slices of fire-roasted poblano peppers simmered in a decadent cream sauce with tomatoes and a hint of garlic.

Enjoy this dish as a side with your favorite entrée or as a filling for your favorite taco.

YIELD: 4 SERVINGS

4 poblano chiles, fire roasted, stemmed, seeded and peeled (page 18)

2 tsp (10 ml) olive oil

1 white onion, juliened

4 garlic cloves, minced

2 Roma tomatoes, diced

1 cup (240 ml) Mexican crema (page 15) or crème fraîche

Salt and pepper

Cut the poblano chile into ¼-inch (6 mm)-thick strips and set aside.

Heat the olive oil in a medium-size sauté pan over medium-high heat until shimmering. Stir the onions into the pan and sauté for 5 minutes, until just soft. Add the garlic and cook for an additional 2 minutes, until the garlic begins to turn a golden brown. Add the Roma tomatoes and poblano strips and cook for 5 minutes, until the tomatoes soften.

Reduce the heat to medium-low and stir in the crema. Season with salt and pepper to taste. Cook for an additional 3–4 minutes, until the cream mixture just begins to simmer.

Remove from the heat and serve warm.

Escabeche de Cebolla

YUCATÁN PICKLED RED ONIONS

The pickled red onion is essential in Yucatán cuisine and accompanies many traditional dishes, including Cochinita Pibil (page 66). It is so easy to make and brightens up any dish with its sweet acidity and bright, hot pink color.

YIELD: 1 CUP (150 G)

1 red onion, peeled and thinly sliced

1 tsp salt

1½ cups (360 ml) fresh lime juice

1 tsp dried oregano, preferably Mexican

½ tsp ground cumin

Place the red onion and salt in a nonreactive bowl and stir in the lime juice. Set the mixture aside and let the ingredients marinate for 30 minutes, until the onions begin to turn a bright pink color. Stir in the oregano and cumin and cover and refrigerate for a minimum of 4 hours before serving.

Jalapeños en Escabeche

PICKLED JALAPEÑO PEPPERS

This is a very simple and quick side dish that is seen throughout Mexico.

At the restaurants, we pickle jalapeños and carrots by the bucketful and serve them on a variety of dishes. The jalapeños take on an almost sweet flavor in the acidic vinegar and taste amazing, even eaten on their own. I indulge in them almost like candy and can rarely resist the temptation to grab a quick bite every time I see them.

YIELD: 2 CUPS (340 G)

½ lb (227 g) fresh jalapeño peppers

6 carrots

2 tbsp (30 ml) canola oil

12 garlic cloves, peeled

2 cups (480 ml) white vinegar

2 sprigs fresh thyme

½ tbsp (2 g) sugar

Salt

2 bay leaves

Cut the jalapeños in half lengthwise and set aside. Peel the carrots and cut into diagonal ¼-inch (6 mm)-thick coins.

Meanwhile, heat the oil in a large sauté pan over medium heat until shimmering.

Add the jalapeños, carrots and garlic to the pan and cook for 10 minutes, stirring often.

Stir in the vinegar, thyme sprigs, sugar, salt and bay leaves. Bring the mixture to a simmer and cook for an additional 10 minutes. Remove from the heat and set aside to cool. Store in an airtight container in the refrigerator until ready to use.

Note: Jalapeños en Escabeche is also excellent pickled in jars and used year-round.

Elote

MEXICAN GRILLED CORN

On the streets of Mexico, you can often see vendors selling beautiful ears of corn charred on the grill, rubbed with mayonnaise, and dusted with cheese and spices.

Because my family is not a huge fan of mayonnaise, I typically replace it with tangy Mexican crema. The last-minute sprinkling of cheese, ancho chile powder and a squeeze of lime add the finishing elements that make Elote a tasty, traditional Mexican snack or an excellent summertime side dish.

YIELD: 4 SERVINGS

4 large ears fresh corn

½ cup (110 g) mayonnaise or Mexican crema (page 15)

1 cup (180 g) crumbled Mexican cotija or Romano cheese

4 tsp (3 g) cilantro leaves, chopped

4 tsp (10 g) ancho chile powder

1 tsp salt

1 lime, quartered

Gently peel back the outside husks of the corn to expose the kernels. Remove the silk threads but leave the husks attached at the base of the cob. Tie the husks together with a piece of kitchen twine or an extra piece of corn husk.

Place the corn in a pot of water or the kitchen sink and soak for 30 minutes to 1 hour.

Preheat an outdoor grill or grill pan over medium-high heat. Brush the grill grates lightly with olive oil to prevent the corn from sticking. Remove the corn from the water and lay directly on the grill, keeping as much of the corn husks away from the flames as possible. Cook the corn for 15–20 minutes, turning every 5 minutes, until the corn kernels are slightly blackened and tender when pierced with a paring knife.

Remove the corn from the grill and brush lightly with the mayonnaise or crema. Place the cheese in a shallow baking dish and gently roll the corn in it until thoroughly coated on all sides. Repeat the process with all ears of corn.

Place the corn on a serving platter and sprinkle evenly with the chopped cilantro, ancho chile powder and salt. Serve with lime wedges.

Note: Cotija cheese can now be found in many local markets, but Romano cheese makes a good substitute if necessary.

Frijole Refritos

REFRIED BLACK BEANS

We serve these black beans on the side of many of our entrées at both restaurants. The flavor is so rich that it is hard to believe they are made with canola oil and not lard. The secret is to sauté the onions over medium-low heat and allow their natural sugar to come out and not burn. The sautéed garlic helps give the beans a slightly sweet flavor. As with most of the dishes in this book, don't skimp on the salt as it helps amplify the flavor.

YIELD: 2 CUPS (400 G)

3 tbsp (45 ml) canola oil

½ cup (65 g) thinly sliced white onion

4 garlic cloves, chopped

2 cups (402 g) cooked black beans, Frijoles de la Olla (page 131) or canned (including the liquid)

Salt

Queso fresco

Heat 2 tablespoons (30 ml) of the canola oil in a large sauté pan or Dutch oven over medium-low heat, until the oil is hot and begins to shimmer. Add the sliced onions and cook, stirring often, until the onions have softened and begin to turn a light golden color. Stir in the garlic and cook for 3–4 minutes, until the garlic has lost all of its bitter taste but has not yet begun to brown. Stir the beans into the mixture and heat for 1 minute.

Remove from the heat and set aside to cool slightly. Using a blender or an immersion blender, blend the bean mixture until relatively smooth. Be careful to leave a few chunks so that the mixture doesn't resemble baby food.

Heat the remaining 1 tablespoon (15 ml) canola oil in a large sauté pan or Dutch oven over medium-low heat until the oil is hot. Pour the pureed bean mixture into the pan and simmer, stirring frequently, for 20 minutes, until it has reduced and is relatively thick. Season with salt and serve sprinkled with queso fresco.

Arroz Poblano

POBLANO RICE

In Mexican cuisine, there are many types of rice, but Arroz Poblano is by far my favorite. Fire-roasting and peeling the peppers adds a nice smoky flavor.

I prefer to finish the cooking process in the oven, but you can finish the rice on the stove top if you wish.

Arroz Poblano goes well with both grilled meat and fish.

YIELD: 6 SERVINGS

1 cup (211 g) long-grain white rice

2 poblano chile peppers, fire roasted, stemmed and seeded (page 18)

½ white onion, dry roasted (page 18)

2 garlic cloves, dry roasted and peeled (page 18)

1 tsp salt

½ cup (120 ml) hot water

2 tbsp (30 ml) canola oil

1 cup (240 ml) vegetable or chicken broth

2 fresh cilantro sprigs

Preheat the oven to 350°F (177°C).

Place the rice in a large bowl and cover with cool water; let soak for 5 minutes. Drain the rice using a colander and rinse under cold water for 2–3 minutes, or until the water runs clear. Shake the colander to remove excess water and let it sit in the sink for 3–4 minutes to continue draining.

Puree the roasted poblano chiles, onion, garlic, salt and hot water in a blender for 1–2 minutes, until the mixture is extremely smooth.

Heat the canola oil in a medium-size saucepan until hot and the oil begins to shimmer. Add the rice to the pan all at once and cook over medium heat, stirring often, for approximately 3 minutes, until the rice begins to brown slightly.

Stir in the pureed ingredients along with the broth. Continue to stir and allow the mixture to come to a full boil. Taste and season with additional salt if necessary.

Transfer the mixture to a large baking dish and top with the fresh cilantro. Cover the dish tightly with a lid or aluminum foil and bake in the oven for 30–35 minutes, until the rice is cooked through and slightly al dente. Remove from the oven and fluff with a fork prior to serving.

Frijoles a la Charro

SPICY BACON PINTO BEANS

Frijoles a la Charro (cowboy beans) is a spicy bean dish named after the charros, or Mexican horsemen. It's incredibly simple to make and the natural tenderness of the pinto beans is enhanced by the textural contrast of the crisp, smoky bacon. I've used two serrano peppers in this recipe, but feel free to add more if you prefer a little extra spice.

Frijoles a la Charro makes a great meal by itself, or as a side dish for grilled meat.

YIELD: 5 CUPS (1 KG)

1 lb (454 g) dried pinto beans, rinsed and free of any debris

1 white onion, quartered

4 garlic cloves

6 slices bacon, uncooked and chopped

½ small white onion, diced

3 garlic cloves, minced

2 serrano chile peppers, diced

2 Roma tomatoes, diced

1 tsp salt

½ cup (20 g) cilantro leaves, chopped

Place the beans in a large stockpot or clay olla and cover with plenty of water; soak for 6 hours or overnight. Drain and discard the soaking liquid. Return the soaked beans to the stockpot along with the quartered onion and whole garlic cloves. Add enough water to the pot to rise approximately 2 inches (5 cm) above the beans.

Place the pot over medium-low heat and simmer, uncovered, for 2 hours, stirring occasionally, until the beans are tender. Check and stir the beans every 15–20 minutes to ensure that they are covered in water and not sticking to the bottom of the pan. Add more water to the pan if necessary to ensure that all of the beans are always covered with water.

Once the beans are fully cooked, remove from the heat and discard the onion and garlic.

Heat a large saucepan or Dutch oven over medium-high heat. Stir in the bacon and cook until it is crispy and golden brown. Stir in the diced onion, minced garlic and serrano peppers and cook for 3 minutes. Add the tomatoes and cook for 5 minutes, or until they have softened. Add the cooked beans and their cooking liquid to the pan and stir to thoroughly combine. Season with salt. Cook for 8–10 minutes longer until the flavors have blended and most of the liquid has evaporated.

Taste and season with additional salt if desired. Serve hot, garnished with chopped cilantro leaves.

Frijoles de la Olla

CLAY POT BEANS

Frijoles de la Olla are an essential item at both restaurants and at my home, although I cook them in a metal pot rather than a clay one. Topped with queso fresco, they make an excellent meal by themselves, or they can be used as a side dish or blended to make Frijoles Refritos (page 126).

Once you make them and find out just how delicious and easy they are, you may never go back to buying canned beans again.

YIELD: 10 CUPS (2 KG)

---

2 lb (907 g) black beans, rinsed and free of any debris

1 white onion, quartered

4 garlic cloves

Salt

Queso fresco

Place the rinsed beans in a large stockpot or clay olla and cover with plenty of water; soak for 6 hours or overnight. Drain the beans and return to the stockpot along with the onion and garlic. Pour enough water into the pot to rise approximately 2 inches (5 cm) above the beans.

Place the pot over medium-low heat and simmer, uncovered, for 2 hours, stirring occasionally, until the beans are tender. Check and stir the beans every 15-20 minutes to ensure that they are covered in water and not sticking to the bottom of the pan. Add more water to the pan if necessary to ensure that all of the beans are always covered with water.

Once the beans are fully cooked, remove from the heat and discard the onion and garlic. Season to taste with salt and ladle into serving bowls or plates with a slotted spoon. Top with the queso fresco.

six

Dulce

SWEET ENDINGS

When I was first opening Zapoteca, a chef mentor once told me that the two most important dishes of a meal are the appetizer and the dessert.

The appetizer, because it is the first impression that a guest has when eating your food, and the dessert, because it is the last moment that you will have to wow them before they leave.

Because of this, many of the desserts at the restaurants are filled with countless components to increase the wow factor.

The desserts in this chapter are based on the desserts at the restaurants, but with much simpler details to allow you to spend more time with your guests and family rather than in the kitchen. The wow factor, however, was not omitted.

Flan de Vainilla

CLASSIC MEXICAN VANILLA FLAN

Flan is a customary custard dessert served throughout Mexico. My restaurateur partner, Sergio, has made this recipe for his family for years and it is by far the best vanilla flan that I have ever eaten.

It is incredibly simple, and the caramelized sugar creates a golden, syrupy topping. Don't be put off, as I originally was, by the use of canned evaporated and sweetened condensed milks. They work very well here and the finished dessert is incredibly creamy and silky.

YIELD: 2 (6 INCH [15 CM]) ROUND FLANS

2 cups (383 g) plus 2 tbsp (24 g) sugar

8 eggs, lightly beaten

2 (13 oz [396 ml]) cans evaporated milk

2 (14 oz [397 ml]) cans sweetened condensed milk

4 tbsp (60 ml) vanilla extract

Fresh fruit, for garnish (optional)

Preheat the oven to 325°F (163°C).

Place 2 cups (383 g) of the sugar in a medium-size sauté pan over medium-low heat. Slowly melt the sugar until it is a golden brown, swirling the pan when needed to melt evenly. Resist the temptation to stir the sugar, as this will cause the caramel to be clumpy.

Carefully pour the caramel into two 6-inch (15 cm)-round cake pans and evenly coat the bottom. Set aside.

In a large mixing bowl, whisk together the eggs, evaporated milk, sweetened condensed milk, vanilla extract and remaining 2 tablespoons (24 g) sugar. Pour the mixture into the prepared cake pans.

Place the cake pans in an extra-large baking dish and pour 1–2 inches (2.5–5 cm) of hot water around them. Bake for 45–50 minutes, or until the flan has set.

Remove the flans from the water bath and chill for 2 hours until cool. Invert the pans onto a serving platter, allowing the caramel to flow over the custard. Serve, garnished with fresh fruit, if desired.

Pastel de Chocolate y Chile Ancho

FLOURLESS CHOCOLATE ANCHO CAKE

Ancho chile pepper is my favorite dried chile, not only for its almost sweet, nutty flavor but also for its versatility. It can be used in almost everything from poultry or meat dishes to even, as in this recipe, dessert.

Because this cake has no flour, it is a great option to serve at a dinner party, if you are concerned that one of your guests could have an issue with gluten. The pepper complements the chocolate very well and provides a subtle amount of heat.

YIELD: 6-8 SERVINGS

1 tbsp (7 g) cocoa powder

2 tsp (5 g) ancho chile powder

7 oz (198 g) unsalted butter, cut into large chunks, at room temperature plus 1 tbsp (14 g) for the pan

1½ cups (270 g) good-quality semisweet chocolate

5 large eggs, at room temperature

1 cup (192 g) sugar

Fresh fruit, for garnish (optional)

Preheat the oven to 350°F (177°C).

Combine the cocoa powder with 1 teaspoon of the ancho chile powder.

Butter a 9-inch (23 cm) springform pan with 1 tablespoon (14 g) of the butter and dust with the cocoa powder–chile mixture. Lightly tap the sides of the pan to remove any excess. Wrap the outside of the pan completely with aluminum foil, as it will be baking in a water bath.

Place the chocolate in a medium-size bowl or pan and melt, stirring often, in a double boiler over medium-high heat. Stir in the remaining 1 teaspoon ancho chile powder and the remaining 7 ounces (198 g) butter until the butter is completely melted and thoroughly combined with the chocolate. Remove from the heat.

In a large mixing bowl, whisk together the eggs and sugar. Slowly stir the egg mixture into the melted chocolate until completely combined.

Pour the batter into the prepared pan and tightly cover the top with aluminum foil. Place the pan in a large roasting pan and pour 2 inches (5 cm) of water around the cake pan. Bake in the preheated oven for 1 hour. Remove the pan from the water bath and cool completely before slicing and serving.

Once cool, slice and serve, garnished with fresh fruit, if desired.

Churros con Cajeta y Tequila

SWEET FRIED LATIN DOUGHNUTS WITH GOAT'S MILK TEQUILA CARAMEL SAUCE

Churros are sold throughout Mexico by street vendors. The vendor typically squeezes the dough out into a pan of hot oil, cooks it, dusts it in cinnamon and sugar and then serves the churro to you either by itself or in a paper bag.

At the restaurants, we often serve our churros alongside a creamy and delicious goat's milk and tequila caramel sauce. The goat's milk adds an earthy component to this sweet ending.

YIELD: 10 CHURROS

GOAT'S MILK TEQUILA CARAMEL SAUCE
¼ tsp baking soda

1 tbsp (15 ml) warm water

1 qt (1 L) goat's milk

1 cup (192 g) sugar

2 tbsp (30 ml) light corn syrup

1 vanilla bean, split

2 tbsp (30 ml) silver tequila (I recommend Herradura Silver)

CINNAMON-SUGAR
½ cup (96 g) sugar

1 tsp ground cinnamon

CHURROS
1 cup (240 ml) water

2½ tbsp (30 g) sugar

½ tsp salt

2 tbsp (30 ml) canola oil

1 cup (125 g) all-purpose flour

2 qts (2 L) canola oil, for frying

GOAT'S MILK TEQUILA CARAMEL SAUCE
Stir the baking soda into the warm water to dissolve. Set aside.

Combine the goat's milk, sugar, light corn syrup and vanilla bean in a medium-size saucepan. Bring to a low simmer over medium heat, stirring often. Remove from the heat and stir in the baking soda–water mixture, stirring constantly, until the frothing subsides.

Return to the heat and bring to a simmer. Cook for 1 hour, stirring every 5 minutes, until the mixture turns a pale, golden color. Begin stirring the caramel constantly and cook for an additional 15 minutes, until it is a rich, golden brown. Remove from the heat and stir in the tequila. Set aside to cool slightly while you prepare the churros. Remove the vanilla bean before serving.

CINNAMON-SUGAR
Combine the sugar and cinnamon in a shallow bowl and set aside.

CHURROS
Combine the water, sugar, salt and canola oil in a medium-size saucepan and bring to a boil over medium-high heat. Remove from the heat and stir in the flour. Spoon the mixture into a pastry bag fitted with a large star tip.

Heat the canola oil in a large, heavy saucepan or Dutch oven until extremely hot and shimmering (375°F [191°C]).

Pipe approximately 4 inches (10 cm) of dough into the hot oil, using kitchen shears to snip the end. Be careful not to overcrowd the pan, as you will only be able to cook 3–4 churros at one time. Fry the churros in the oil, turning once, for approximately 4 minutes until golden brown. Use a slotted spoon to remove from the oil and place on a paper towel–lined platter to drain. Repeat with the remaining dough.

Roll the warm churros in the prepared cinnamon-sugar and serve with the warm caramel sauce.

Note: If you do not have a pastry bag with a star tip, a plastic storage bag with the corner cut off will work fine as a replacement.

Plátanos a la Brasa con Helado de Ron

GRILLED BANANAS WITH SEA SALT AND RUM ICE CREAM

In addition to its amazing tequila, Mexico produces some excellent rum, which is highlighted in this recipe.

This dessert is incredibly simple to make and is perfect for a summer dinner party or barbecue, as the ice cream can be made in advance and the bananas are quick to prepare on the grill. The creamy rum ice cream balances the sweetness of the bananas and the sea salt flakes add a great, unexpected element.

YIELD: 4 SERVINGS

RUM ICE CREAM
¾ cup (144 g) sugar
6 egg yolks
2 cups (473 ml) milk
2 cups (473 ml) heavy cream
1 tbsp (15 ml) vanilla extract
⅓ cup (80 ml) dark rum, preferably Mexican

GRILLED BANANAS
1 tbsp (15 ml) olive oil
1 cup (201 g) piloncillo or light brown sugar
2 tsp (5 g) ground cinnamon
4 underripe, firm bananas
1 tbsp (15 ml) lemon juice
½ tsp sea salt flakes

RUM ICE CREAM
Add the sugar and egg yolks to a mixing bowl or the bowl of a stand mixer, and mix for 2 minutes until it turns a light yellow color. Stir in the milk. Transfer to a saucepan and bring to a low simmer over medium heat. Continue simmering for 10 minutes, until it thickens and coats the back of the spoon when stirred. Remove from the heat and pour through a fine-mesh strainer. Stir in the heavy cream, vanilla extract and rum. Cover with plastic wrap and chill for 1 hour.

Pour into an ice cream maker and prepare according to the manufacturer's directions.

GRILLED BANANAS
Preheat an outdoor grill or grill pan over medium-high heat. Brush the grill grates lightly with olive oil to prevent the bananas from sticking.

Combine the piloncillo and cinnamon and place in a shallow mixing bowl. Set aside.

Peel the bananas and cut in half lengthwise and then in half widthwise. Lightly drizzle with lemon juice. Toss the bananas in the sugar-cinnamon mixture and place on the gill, cut side down. Grill for 6 minutes, turning once. Remove the bananas from the grill, sprinkle with sea salt and serve with the rum ice cream.

Note: Be sure to use firm bananas, as overripe ones will fall apart on the grill.

Tarta de Limón

LIME TARTS WITH ANCHO GRAHAM CRUST AND AGAVE WHIPPED CREAM

Limes, chile peppers and agave nectar are three products available throughout Mexico. This simple tart recipe utilizes these three key ingredients to create a refreshing lime dessert that is easy to make and elegant enough to enjoy at any gathering.

YIELD: 6 (4 INCH [10 CM]) TARTS

ANCHO GRAHAM CRUST
¼ cup (48 g) sugar
Zest from 1 lime
1 tsp ancho chile powder
1½ cups (135 g) graham cracker crumbs
6 tbsp (86 g) unsalted butter, melted

LIME FILLING
2 egg yolks
1 (14 oz [397 g]) can sweetened condensed milk
½ cup (120 ml) lime juice

AGAVE WHIPPED CREAM
2 tbsp (24 g) sugar
1 tbsp (15 ml) agave nectar
1 cup (240 ml) heavy whipping cream

Zest of 1 lime, for garnish

ANCHO GRAHAM CRUST
Preheat the oven to 350°F (177°C).

Blend the sugar, lime zest and ancho chile powder in a blender until smooth. Transfer to a large mixing bowl and stir in the graham cracker crumbs and melted butter. Mix until thoroughly combined.

Divide the graham cracker mixture equally among six 4-inch (10 cm) tart pans. Press down so that the crumbs are flat against the bottom of the tin and rise slightly on the sides. Bake in the preheated oven for 10 minutes. Set the crusts aside to cool while you prepare the filling.

LIME FILLING
Whisk the egg yolks with the sweetened condensed milk until thoroughly combined, and then stir in the lime juice. Pour the custard evenly among the prepared tart tins. Bake in the preheated oven for 15 minutes. Remove from the oven and chill for 1 hour, or until set.

AGAVE WHIPPED CREAM
Place the sugar, agave nectar and whipping cream in a large stainless steel bowl or stand mixer. Mix until soft peaks form.

Remove the tarts from the tins and top with the Agave Whipped Cream and sprinkle with the lime zest.

Paletas de Mango con Chile

MANGO-CHILE ICE POPS

There are literally hundreds of different flavors of paleta (ice pops) that you can find throughout Mexico. Mango-chile is one of the most popular and my absolute favorite.

If you've never eaten a paleta, you've never had an ice pop quite like this. This version is packed full of chunks of fresh mango combined with sweet juice and a hint of chile. If the thought of this combination isn't enough to tempt you, the bright color surely will.

YIELD: 8 ICE POPS

1¼ cups (296 ml) mango juice (Goya is a great option)

¼ cup (48 g) sugar

Juice of 2 limes

½ cup (120 ml) water

1 large mango, peeled, seeded and diced

1 tsp ancho chile powder

Place the mango juice, sugar, lime juice and water in a heavy-bottomed saucepan and bring to a simmer over medium heat. Transfer to a bowl and refrigerate until completely cool.

Combine the diced mango and ancho chile powder with the chilled mixture and pour into 8 ice pop molds. Place a popsicle stick into each mold and chill for 6 hours, or until completely frozen. Remove from the molds and serve.

Note : If not everyone in your family enjoys the spice, omit the chile in a few of the pops. If you can't find mango juice, pineapple juice makes a great substitute.

Bunuelos con Miel de Anis

MEXICAN FRITTERS WITH CITRUS AND ANISE-SPICED HONEY

Bunuelos are a special treat in Mexico, typically enjoyed around the holiday season. These puffy and crispy round discs of dough are first lightly fried and then dusted with a sweet cinnamon-sugar mixture before being drizzled with citrus and anise-spiced honey.

The addition of the citrus and anise honey, rather than the traditional anise syrup, adds a little flair to this simple and tasty treat.

YIELD: 20 BUNELOS

CITRUS AND ANISE HONEY

1 orange

2 cups (473 ml) honey

2 bay leaves

1 cinnamon stick

2 whole star anise or ½ tsp anise seeds

CINNAMON-SUGAR

½ cup (96 g) sugar

2 tsp (5 g) ground cinnamon

BUNUELOS

3 cups (375 g) all-purpose flour

1 tsp baking powder

1 tsp salt

1 tsp sugar

¾ cup (177 ml) whole milk

¼ cup (57 g) unsalted butter

1 tsp orange liqueur

2 eggs, beaten

2 cups (480 ml) canola oil, for frying

CITRUS AND ANISE HONEY

Using a paring knife or vegetable peeler, remove the peel from the orange. Place in a saucepan along with the honey, bay leaves, cinnamon stick and anise. Heat the mixture over low heat and allow the honey to steep for 10 minutes. Remove from the heat and cool at room temperature. Strain the honey mixture through a fine-mesh strainer, discarding any large particles. Reserve the spiced honey.

CINNAMON-SUGAR

Combine the cinnamon and sugar in a bowl. Set aside.

BUNUELOS

Combine the flour, baking powder, salt and sugar in a large mixing bowl. Set aside.

Heat the milk, butter and orange liqueur in a heavy-bottomed saucepan over medium heat. Bring the mixture to a simmer and remove from the heat. Gradually whisk in the beaten eggs, being careful to only add a small amount at a time to prevent the eggs from cooking.

Add the egg and milk mixture to the dry ingredients, and thoroughly combine. On a lightly floured surface, knead the dough for 3–4 minutes, until the mixture forms a smooth ball. Divide the dough into 20 equal-size balls. Press the balls between the palms of your hand to form a disc. Place the discs onto a lightly oiled tray while you work with the remaining dough.

Place the discs on the floured surface and use a rolling pin to roll into very thin 6-inch (15 cm) tortillas.

Heat the canola oil in a heavy-bottomed sauté pan over medium-high heat until shimmering. Gently place the bunuelo in the oil and fry for approximately 3 minutes, turning once, until golden brown. Remove the bunuelo from the oil and place on a paper towel–lined platter to drain and cool while you fry the others.

Sprinkle with the cinnamon-sugar and serve with the anise honey.

Helado de Maíz

SWEET CORN ICE CREAM WITH SALTED CARAMEL CORN

Corn is an indispensable component in the Mexican diet, and this decadent ice cream utilizes it in a slightly unusual way.

Corn is combined with sweet cream to form a perfectly smooth and silky ice cream with a subtle corn taste reminiscent of summer. The addition of crisp caramel corn takes the dessert to a new level, adding a balanced textural contrast and making it a beautiful dish for summer entertaining.

YIELD: 1 QUART (1 L)

CARAMEL CORN
4 cups (28 g) popped popcorn

1 tsp canola oil or spray

¼ cup (50 g) light brown sugar

2 tbsp (30 ml) light corn syrup

2 tbsp (29 g) unsalted butter

¼ tsp salt

¼ tsp baking powder

¼ tsp vanilla extract

Sea salt

SWEET CORN ICE CREAM
4 ears fresh corn

2 cups (473 ml) whole milk

2 cups (473 ml) heavy cream

1 vanilla bean, split

¾ cup (144 g) sugar

6 egg yolks

CARAMEL CORN
Preheat the oven to 250°F (121°C).

Place the popcorn on a lightly oiled, large baking dish and put in the preheated oven while you prepare the caramel.

Combine the brown sugar, corn syrup, butter and salt in a medium-size sauté pan. Bring to a simmer over medium heat, stirring constantly. Reduce the heat to low and continue to cook for approximately 10 minutes, until the sugar melts. Remove from the heat and stir in the baking powder and vanilla extract.

Pour the caramel evenly over the warm popcorn. Place the mixture in the oven and cook for 30–45 minutes, stirring every 15 minutes. Remove from the oven, spread on parchment paper to cool and sprinkle lightly with sea salt. Once completely cool, break apart and store in an airtight container.

SWEET CORN ICE CREAM
Using a sharp knife, remove the kernels from the corn and place in a large, heavy-bottomed saucepan along with the cobs. Stir in the milk, heavy cream, vanilla bean and ½ cup (96 g) of the sugar and bring to a simmer over medium heat. Simmer for 2 minutes, stirring constantly. Remove and discard the corncobs and vanilla bean. Allow the mixture to cool for 5 minutes and then blend to a smooth puree in a blender. Return the mixture to the same saucepan and bring to a simmer. Remove from the heat.

Place the egg yolks and remaining ¼ cup (48 g) sugar in a large bowl and whisk thoroughly. Slowly drizzle in ½ cup (120 ml) of the pureed mixture while whisking continuously. Repeat with another ½ cup (120 ml) of the milk mixture. Pour the egg mixture into the saucepan with the milk and heat over medium heat, stirring constantly, for 10 minutes, until the mixture thickens and coats the back of the spoon when stirred.

Strain the mixture through a fine-mesh strainer, discarding the solids, and chill for 4 hours. Place in the bowl of an ice cream maker and freeze according to the manufacturer's directions.

Once frozen, spoon into bowls and top with the Caramel Corn.

Helado de Chocolate con Jalapeño

CHOCOLATE JALAPEÑO ICE CREAM

Chocolate and jalapeño are two ingredients synonymous with Mexican cuisine. In this dessert, these two bold flavors are combined in a luscious ice cream with a creamy, rich texture and hint of spice.

Garnish with a slice of jalapeño to further accentuate the spice level and create a beautiful presentation.

YIELD: 1 QUART (1 L)

2 cups (473 ml) whole milk

1 cup (237 ml) heavy cream

6 tbsp (72 g) sugar

1 jalapeño pepper, stemmed and thinly sliced

6 egg yolks

10 oz (284 g) bittersweet chocolate chips

Combine the milk, heavy cream, sugar and jalapeño in a large saucepan and bring to a simmer over medium heat. Simmer for 5 minutes, stirring constantly. Remove from the heat and let cool for 5 minutes. Once cool, remove and discard the jalapeño pepper.

Whisk the egg yolks together in a large mixing bowl. Slowly drizzle in ½ cup (120 ml) of the milk mixture while whisking continuously. Repeat with another ½ cup (120 ml) of the milk mixture. Pour the egg mixture into the saucepan with the milk and heat over medium heat, stirring constantly, for 10 minutes, until the mixture thickens and coats the back of the spoon when stirred. Whisk in the chocolate pieces and stir until they have completely melted.

Strain the mixture through a fine-mesh strainer, discarding the solids, and chill for 4 hours. Place in the bowl of an ice cream maker and freeze according to the manufacturer's directions.

seven

Salsas y Guacamoles

SALSAS AND GUACAMOLES

Salsa is the cornerstone of a Mexican kitchen, and a genius one at that. The simple addition of salsa to a dish can transform it from ordinary to something completely different and utterly unforgettable.

Salsa, the Spanish word for "sauce", can be made with a variety of ingredients but almost always includes some type of chile, either dried or fresh. The traditional way to make salsa is with a molcajete and tejolote, but these days more and more chefs opt for a simpler preparation using a blender or food processor. At Zapoteca, I use both depending on the type of sauce. Either of these ways is fantastic and will leave you with a great, although different, flavor.

A good salsa should have a complex depth of flavor balanced with a mix of acidity, heat and, of course, my favorite, saltiness. As with many sauces, each salsa has a specific function: some serve to simply be enjoyed with a crisp corn chip, while others serve to flavor meats and tacos.

At the restaurants, and often in this book, I pair a particular salsa with a specific dish because of the flavor and balance it creates with the finished item. I encourage you to try these pairings, but don't be afraid to experiment with different pairings to see the flavor it creates.

This chapter also includes various types of fresh guacamoles. If you've ever tried fresh guacamole versus store-bought guacamole, you know that there is no comparison between the two. Guacamole is so easy to make that once you make it for the first time, I'm sure it will become a staple in your kitchen, and I hope you make it again and again.

Salsa Roja

WARM TOMATO, GARLIC AND SERRANO CHILE SALSA

We have been serving Salsa Roja since day one at both restaurants and to this day, it still remains a favorite among the guests and me.

It is such a simple, rustic and versatile salsa that can be served with grilled meats or eggs or even eaten plain with salted corn chips. Frying the sauce at the last minute before serving is traditional and adds an extra dimension of flavor to this already bold, spicy sauce. The flavors are so pronounced that you would never guess that it contains only three primary ingredients.

YIELD: 3 CUPS (700 G)

4 garlic cloves, dry roasted and peeled (page 18)

3 fresh serrano chiles, dry roasted and stemmed (page 18)

8 fresh Roma tomatoes, dry roasted (page 18)

2 tbsp (30 ml) canola oil

Salt to taste

Combine the dry roasted garlic cloves, serrano chiles and tomatoes in a blender or food processor and pulse 4–5 times until they are broken up and coarsely chopped.

Heat the oil in a heavy, medium-size saucepan over medium-high heat. When the oil is hot and begins to shimmer, pour the salsa into the pan and stir immediately. Be careful, as the salsa will splatter.

Fry the salsa for 2–3 minutes, stirring constantly, until it thickens and begins to darken. Salt to taste and serve while warm with tortilla chips.

Note: If you prefer a less spicy salsa, remove the seeds and ribs from inside the chiles after roasting. Jalapeños may be used if you can't find or don't like fresh serranos.

Salsa Verde

ROASTED TOMATILLO SALSA

If you've been to Mexico or frequent traditional Mexican restaurants in the US, chances are you've seen Salsa Verde served either alone or alongside your favorite taco. The tomatillos give this dish not only its pronounced green color but also a slight citrus flavor, and the jalapeños add just a touch of heat.

This salsa goes amazingly well with chicken or pork, or you can eat it as I do, warm with fresh tortilla chips.

YIELD: 2 CUPS (473 G)

10 tomatillos

2 jalapeño chiles

2 garlic cloves, unpeeled

½ medium white onion, quartered

1 bunch cilantro, stemmed and coarsely chopped

2 tsp (10 g) salt

Gently peel the outside husks and stems of the tomatillos and discard. Rinse the peeled tomatillos under cool water and pat dry with a paper towel. Place in a cast-iron skillet or heavy-bottomed sauté pan and dry roast until blackened on all sides. Be careful not to overcook the tomatillos or they will burst in the pan and release their sweet, tangy flavor.

Repeat the dry roasting process with the jalapeños, unpeeled garlic cloves and white onion. Once they're all evenly blackened, remove from the pan and cut the top stems off of the jalapeño peppers and peel the skins off the garlic cloves.

Combine all of the dry roasted ingredients in a blender or food processor and pulse 2–4 times until broken up and roughly chopped. Add the cilantro and salt to the mixture and quickly pulse another 4–6 times until thoroughly blended and chopped. Season to taste with additional salt if desired. Serve immediately while still warm with tortilla chips or on your favorite taco.

Note: In Mexico, tomatillos are also called tomate verde and are considered a staple. When choosing a tomatillo, look for a smaller sized fruit with tight, unshriveled husks. Avoid the larger tomatillos as they can be very bitter.

Salsa Mexicana

FRESH TOMATO AND ONION SALSA

If there is one recipe in this cookbook that you should include in your regular cooking repertoire, this is the one. It is light, flavorful and above all, extremely versatile. Salsa Mexicana, is incredibly simple because it is made with only a handful of ingredients, including fresh tomatoes, hot chile peppers, onion, cilantro and lime.

The fresh flavors complement any taco or grilled meat extremely well. Be sure to salt the dish just before serving as salting too early will cause the tomatoes to release their natural juices and make the salsa runny.

YIELD: 1 CUP (240 G)

2 serrano chiles, seeded and finely diced

3 Roma tomatoes, diced

¾ cup (114 g) diced white onion

1 cup (40 g) cilantro leaves, finely chopped, plus extra for garnish

1 tbsp (15 ml) fresh lime juice

½ tbsp (7 ml) olive oil

½ tsp salt

Combine all the ingredients, excluding the salt, in a medium-size bowl and toss to combine thoroughly.

Refrigerate until needed and season with salt just before serving to prevent the tomato from sweating excess water. Garnish with additional cilantro and serve.

Note: Salsa Mexicana is also referred to as Pico de Gallo. The origin of the name pico de gallo is not clear and there are many speculations behind why this salsa is actually called "rooster's beak." One story is that the small pieces of tomato and pepper resemble something that a rooster pecked.

Sikil Pak

MAYAN PUMPKIN SEED SALSA

Sikil Pak originated in the Yucatán and is a rich salsa that uses some of the most traditional flavors of the Mayan culture: pumpkin seeds, tomatoes and chiles.

The pumpkin seeds thicken this intense sauce while the tangy flavor is enriched by the sweet tomato and bold heat of the habanero chile. I've created this recipe using only half of a habanero to balance out the flavors without adding too much heat, but feel free to use the full habanero if you prefer a little more spice.

YIELD: 2 CUPS (480 G)

1 cup (140 g) pumpkin seeds, plus extra for garnish

½ fresh habanero chile, dry roasted (page 18)

2 garlic cloves, dry roasted and stemmed (page 18)

2 Roma tomatoes, dry roasted (page 18)

½ cup (20 g) fresh cilantro leaves, chopped

2 tbsp (6 g) finely chopped chives

2 tbsp (30 ml) freshly squeezed lime juice

1 tbsp (15 ml) extra virgin olive oil

¼ cup (60 ml) water

1 tsp orange zest

¾ tsp salt

Tortillas, for serving

Heat a large sauté pan over medium heat. Once the pan is hot, add the pumpkin seeds and cook until they begin to pop and are lightly toasted. Be careful not to burn the seeds as this will make the salsa bitter.

Remove the pumpkin seeds from the pan and place them in a blender or food processor along with the dry roasted habanero, garlic, tomatoes, cilantro, chives and lime juice. Turn the blender or food processor on and gradually add the olive oil in a slow, continuous stream. Add the water in the same way and process for 1 minute, until smooth and thoroughly combined. Stir in the orange zest and season with salt.

Serve with fresh flour tortillas or warm corn tortilla chips.

Note: Although Sikil Pak is typically used as a salsa to dip chips in, it also makes a great accompaniment to grilled meat—especially grilled chicken.

Salsa de Chile de Árbol

SPICY RED CHILE SALSA

Salsa de Chile de Árbol is one of my favorite go-to hot sauces. The fifty chiles de árbol (yes, that's a lot of peppers) give this sauce a fiery kick, while the vinegar adds just the right amount of acidity. I keep it in the refrigerator and use it every time I want to add a little heat to any of my favorite dishes.

YIELD: 2 CUPS (480 G)

50 dried chile de árbol peppers, stemmed, dry roasted and rehydrated (page 18)

2 tbsp (40 g) pumpkin seeds

2 tbsp (40 g) sesame seeds

¼ tsp cumin seeds

4 allspice berries

1 tsp dried oregano, preferably Mexican

2 tsp (10 g) salt

1 tbsp (12 g) sugar

2 garlic cloves, dry roasted and peeled (page 18)

½ cup (118 ml) cider vinegar

¾ cup (180 ml) water

Place the rehydrated chile de árbol peppers in the bowl of a blender.

Heat a heavy-bottomed sauté pan over medium heat. Once hot, toast the pumpkin seeds for 1–2 minutes, until they begin to pop. Remove from the pan and place in the blender with the rehydrated peppers.

Lightly toast the sesame seeds in the same pan for less than 1 minute, quickly remove from the hot pan (as they will continue to toast) and place in the blender along with the remaining ingredients.

Blend all of the ingredients for 5 minutes, or until they are pureed into a smooth paste.

Cover and refrigerate until needed.

Note: Chile de árbol is native to Mexico and has a heat index comparable to that of the cayenne pepper. Thus, use this sauce sparingly because even a little bit can pack a full punch.

Salsa de Naranja y Chipotle

ORANGE CHIPOTLE SALSA

I love the combination of sweetness and spice in this salsa. The oranges create an intense sweetness that perfectly complements the smoky, subtle heat of the chipotle chiles. I've added orange zest along with the traditional orange juice to further intensify the citrus flavor.

Salsa de Naranja y Chipotle makes a great condiment to serve alongside your favorite taco, atop roasted pork or eaten alone with warm tortilla chips.

YIELD: 1 CUP (240 G)

2 chipotle chiles en adobo

6 Roma tomatoes

1 small white onion, quartered

1 bunch fresh cilantro, stems removed, plus more for garnish

4 garlic cloves, dry roasted and peeled (page 18)

Juice of 1 orange

½ tsp orange zest

Salt

In a food processor or blender, combine the chipotle chiles, tomatoes, white onion, cilantro and roasted garlic and blend for 2 minutes until all the vegetables are finely chopped and combined. Slowly add the orange juice and pulse to combine. Transfer the mixture to a large bowl and stir in the orange zest. Season to taste with salt and garnish with fresh cilantro.

Salsa Borracha

DRUNKEN SALSA

Because Salsa Borracha is made with dried chiles rather than fresh, it is not your typical salsa. The dried pasilla chiles help give it a deep earthy, piquant taste while the addition of tequila amps up the flavor even further and pushes it over the top. It goes amazingly well with grilled meat or lamb, but it's not suited to being eaten alone with fresh chips. I love it lightly drizzled over the Adobo-Glazed Chicken Empanadas (page 38).

YIELD: 1½ CUPS (360 G)

1 corn tortilla

2 tomatillos, peeled and dry roasted (page 18)

5 dried pasilla chiles, seeded, stemmed, dry roasted and rehydrated (page 18)

1 garlic clove, dry roasted and peeled (page 18)

¼ white onion, dry roasted (page 18)

¼ cup (60 ml) Herradura Silver tequila

2 tbsp (30 ml) orange juice

2 tbsp (30 ml) canola oil

Salt

Heat a comal or heavy-bottomed sauté pan over medium heat. Once hot, cook the tortilla until lightly blackened on both sides. Place the cooked tortilla in the bowl of a blender or food processor along with the tomatillos, pasilla chiles, garlic, white onion, tequila and orange juice and puree until smooth, approximately 2 minutes.

Heat the canola oil in a sauté pan over medium-high heat until it shimmers, add the salsa and cook for 5 minutes until it thickens and begins to darken. Season with salt.

Salsa de Piña a la Plancha

GRILLED PINEAPPLE SALSA

Grilling pineapple is something we do on a daily basis at both restaurants. Whether adding it to a drink or putting it in a salsa, the grilling process intensifies the sweetness of the pineapple and amps up its flavor with a slightly charred taste.

Adding habanero to this salsa adds my favorite thing: heat. You can eat it alone, with grilled fish or pork or atop Tacos al Pastor (page 30).

YIELD: 2 CUPS (480 G)

---

1 fresh pineapple, peeled, cored and cut into ¼" (6 mm)-thick rings

1 habanero chile, dry roasted, stemmed, seeded and finely diced (page 18)

1 sweet red bell pepper, cored, seeded and finely diced

1 tbsp (2.5 g) cilantro leaves, finely chopped

1 tbsp (15 ml) lime juice

Salt

Heat a grill or heavy-bottomed sauté pan over medium-high heat. Grill the pineapple on both sides until lightly charred. Remove the pineapple from the heat and cut into small ¼-inch (6 mm) chunks. Transfer to a large bowl and gently stir in the diced habanero, bell pepper, cilantro and lime juice. Season to taste with salt. Serve immediately or refrigerate until ready to use.

Note: If pineapples aren't your thing, feel free to substitute fresh mango.

Salsa de Chile Habanero

FIERY HABANERO SALSA

This salsa is a great example of how the habanero chile is used in Yucatecán cuisine. The bright orange color makes it visually stunning, while the intense heat from the chile makes the bold flavor utterly unforgettable. The addition of carrots adds a slight sweetness and creates a brilliant balanced taste.

Drizzle it over Cochinita Pibil (page 66) or on your favorite taco to add a little extra heat.

YIELD: 1½ CUPS (360 G)

---

1 tbsp (15 ml) olive oil

2 carrots, peeled and roughly chopped

2 Roma tomatoes, dry roasted (page 18)

½ white onion, dry roasted (page 18)

4 habanero chiles, dry roasted, stemmed and seeded (page 18)

4 garlic cloves, dry roasted and peeled (page 18)

¼ cup (60 ml) lime juice

¼ cup (60 ml) apple cider vinegar

¼ tsp sugar

1 tsp salt

Heat the olive oil in a heavy-bottomed sauté pan over medium heat. Once the oil is hot and begins to shimmer, stir in the chopped carrots and cook for approximately 7 minutes, or until they begin to soften. Remove the carrots from the heat and place in a blender, along with the dry roasted vegetables, lime juice, apple cider vinegar, sugar and salt. Blend until smooth. Feel free to add a little water (1 tablespoon [15 ml] at a time) if you think the salsa is too thick.

Store covered in the refrigerator until ready to use.

Note: When buying habanero chiles, keep in mind that the orange and yellow peppers are hotter than the green ones.

Salsa Macha

SESAME AND PEANUT SALSA

Mexico is a huge melting pot with ties from all over the world, including Korea and China. This salsa from the Yucatán region is a perfect example of the blending of ingredients typically used in Mexican cooking with the traditional flavors of Asian cuisine.

The mild flavor of the sesame is joined by the piquancy of the chile peppers. I've added just a touch of brown sugar to balance the heat with a little sweetness. It's great with warm tortilla chips or on top of your favorite taco.

YIELD: 2 CUPS (473 G)

1½ cups (355 ml) canola oil

⅓ cup (50 g) peanuts

4 garlic cloves, sliced

1 tbsp (10 g) sesame seeds

20 chiles de árbol, stemmed

2 tbsp (30 ml) cider vinegar

2 tbsp (25 g) piloncillo or light brown sugar

1 tbsp (15 g) salt

Heat the oil in a heavy-bottomed sauté pan over medium heat until the oil shimmers. Sauté the peanuts in the pan for approximately 2 minutes, or until they are slightly toasted. Remove from the pan and place on a plate lined with a paper towel to drain. Sauté the garlic in the same manner and place on the paper towel with the peanuts to drain.

Carefully discard of the oil in the pan and return the pan to the heat, reducing it to low. Lightly toast the sesame seeds, stirring often, until they are a light, golden brown. Place the sesame seeds in the bowl of a blender or food processer and set aside.

Return the pan to the heat and lightly toast the chile de árbol peppers for 2 minutes, until crisp. Place the peppers in the blender or food processor with the sesame seeds and add the peanuts, garlic, cider vinegar, sugar and salt and pulse until all the ingredients are thoroughly chopped and combined.

Set aside to cool. Cover and refrigerate until ready to use.

Note: Salsa Macha has an almost Asian flavor and goes well on tacos, but I also love to use it on sandwiches or to add a punch of heat to pasta.

Guacamole de Aguacate

FRESH AVOCADO GUACAMOLE

At the restaurants, guacamole is by far the most popular appetizer on the menu. My version includes a cilantro-chile paste to stir the avocado chunks in and to ensure that every single bit of avocado is drenched in spicy flavor. Don't skimp on the salt; it's an essential ingredient to bring out all of the zest.

YIELD: 4 CUPS (946 G)

2 tbsp (25 g) finely diced white onion
1 tbsp (3 g) cilantro, finely chopped
1 tbsp (11 g) finely diced jalapeño chiles
1½ tsp (8 g) salt
4 ripe avocados
3 tbsp (30 g) diced Roma tomato
Tortilla chips or Tortillas, for serving

Blend 1 tablespoon (12.5 g) of the diced onion, cilantro, jalapeño and salt together in a molcajete or blender and thoroughly blend until you have a smooth puree. If you are using a blender, you may need to add up to 1 tablespoon (15 ml) of water to help the ingredients blend completely. Place the pureed mixture in a large bowl and set aside.

Cut each avocado in half and discard the seed. Using a butter knife, make 4 evenly spaced lengthwise cuts through the avocado, being careful not to cut through the skin. Make 4 crosswise cuts in the same way. Scoop the diced avocado into the bowl with the puree mixture and repeat with the remaining avocados.

Gently stir the avocado into the puree along with the remaining 1 tablespoon (12.5 g) diced onion and tomato until well blended. Season to taste with salt, if necessary. Serve with warm tortilla chips or tortillas.

Note: When choosing the right avocado, it should slightly give when gently squeezed with the palm of your hand, but not be mushy or extremely soft to the touch. If possible, always choose an avocado with the small brown stem still attached. The stem acts as a plug and allows less air to enter and discolor the avocado.

Variation: Stir ¼ cup (52 g) chilled lobster meat into the guacamole.

Guacamole de Pistacho y Queso de Leche de Cabra

PISTACHIO AND GOAT CHEESE GUACAMOLE

In this dish, the traditional spicy flavors of guacamole are combined with the earthy creaminess of goat cheese and the crunchy texture of pistachios. Together, each individual flavor is intensified and absolutely amazing.

I first served this dish at a function for National Pistachio Day. The result was a huge success, and although it is not on the menu at either restaurant, we continually receive regular requests to make it again and again.

YIELD: 3 CUPS (709 G)

3 ripe avocados

3 Roma tomatoes, dry roasted and diced (page 118)

1 tbsp (2.5 g) cilantro leaves, finely chopped

1 tbsp (11 g) finely diced jalapeño chile

1 tsp salt

½ cup (60 g) crumbled goat cheese

¼ cup (38 g) shelled and toasted pistachios

Tortilla chips, for serving

Cut each avocado in half and discard the large center seed. Using a butter knife, make 4 evenly spaced lengthwise cuts through the avocado, being careful not to cut through the skin of the avocado. Make 4 crosswise cuts in the same way and scoop the diced avocado into a large bowl. Repeat with the remaining avocados.

Add the tomato, cilantro, jalapeño and salt to the bowl and stir to combine. Gently fold in the goat cheese and toasted pistachios.

Serve immediately with warm tortilla chips.

Guacamole de Tocino

CHIPOTLE-AGAVE GLAZED BACON GUACAMOLE

At the restaurants, we make the most amazing brunch. Virtually every dish includes our spicy, sweet Chipotle-Agave Glazed Bacon Guacamole. In this dish, chile-glazed bacon is combined with traditional guacamole to create the ultimate wow experience.

You begin by combing agave syrup, chipotle peppers and roasted garlic to form a sweet and sticky glaze for the crisp bacon. The bacon is stirred into the spicy guacamole to push the dish over the top.

YIELD: 3 CUPS (709 G)

½ cup (120 ml) agave syrup

1 garlic clove, dry roasted and peeled (page 18)

1 chipotle chile en adobo, finely chopped

6 slices of your favorite bacon, cooked

2 tbsp (26 g) finely diced white onion

1 tbsp (3 g) finely chopped cilantro, stemmed

2 tsp (7 g) finely diced jalapeño chile

1 tsp salt

3 ripe avocados

3 tbsp (30 g) diced Roma tomato

Tortilla chips or Tortillas, for serving

Combine the agave syrup, garlic and chipotle pepper in a blender. Gently pulse until you have a smooth syrup. Drizzle over the crisp bacon and roughly chop into small bite-size pieces. Set aside.

Make the chile paste by grinding 1 tablespoon (13 g) of the onion, cilantro, jalapeño and salt in a molcajete or blender, blending until you have a smooth puree. If you are using a blender, you may need to add up to 1 tablespoon (15 ml) of water to help the ingredients blend completely.

Cut each avocado in half and discard the large center seed. Using a butter knife, make 4 evenly spaced lengthwise cuts through the avocado, being careful not to cut through the skin of the avocado. Make 4 crosswise cuts in the same way and scoop the diced avocado into a large bowl. Repeat with the remaining avocados.

Spoon the prepared puree onto the avocado chunks and gently fold, keeping the avocado in as large pieces as possible. Add the tomato, chipotle-agave bacon and remaining 1 tablespoon (13 g) onion and fold in gently. Season to taste with salt. Serve with warm tortilla chips or tortillas.

Note: Be sure to make the bacon extra crispy as it creates a great contrast to the creaminess of the avocado.

eight

Bebidas

BEVERAGES

Many of the recipes in this chapter include one of my favorite drinks, tequila. When I first began researching drinks for the cookbook, I had the good fortune to be invited to tour the Casa Herradura distillery outside of Guadalajara, Mexico.

My first morning there, I woke up to enjoy a horseback ride through the agave fields. The seemingly endless agave plants went on as far as they eye could see, and looked almost like a sea of blue-green water between the rocky hillsides. The ride ended with an authentic breakfast cooked on an open fire and a demonstration of the intricate details and strength it takes to harvest the large, blue agave plant.

The details in making tequila are fascinating, from the cooking of the agave to the detailed fermentation process. Like wine, tequila is fermented in large, stainless steel containers. Herradura's method, however, is somewhat different than most other tequila distilleries as they don't add processed products to complete the fermentation process. Their fermenting drums are left open to allow for open-air fermentation, a process that is truly interesting and amazing to watch.

The final product has a clean, crisp flavor that I could have enjoyed all day.

Margarita de Zapoteca

CLASSIC ZAPOTECA MARGARITA

Any trip to Mexico, or a Mexican restaurant, would not be complete without at least one margarita, and at Zapoteca we are known for our amazing margaritas. This classic is one of our best.

Fresh lime juice is an essential ingredient in this recipe. Don't be tempted to use prepackaged lime juice as the flavor will not be the same.

YIELD: 1 SERVING

---

6 oz (170 ml) ice cubes

1½ oz (45 ml) silver tequila (I recommend Herradura Silver)

½ oz (15 ml) orange liqueur

½ oz (15 ml) agave nectar

1½ oz (45 ml) fresh squeezed lime juice

GARNISH
Salt for rim of glass
Lime wheel

GLASS
Martini

Fill a cocktail shaker with ice and top with the tequila, orange liqueur, agave nectar and fresh squeezed lime juice. Cover the shaker with a tight-fitting lid and shake 12–15 times, until the ice has broken up slightly and the mixture is thoroughly combined.

Place the salt on a flat small plate and gently press the rim of a chilled martini glass into the salt to evenly coat the entire rim. Strain the margarita into the glass and garnish with a lime wheel.

Margarita de Sandia y Habanero

WATERMELON HABANERO MARGARITA

The Watermelon Habanero Margarita is the top-selling drink at both of the restaurants. The sweetness of the watermelon is perfectly balanced with the slight heat of the habanero.

Be careful not to muddle the habanero for too long as the more you muddle the habanero in the shaker, the more intense the heat level will be in the margarita.

YIELD: 1 SERVING

---

3 watermelon cubes, ½" (13 mm) each

1 habanero chile ring

6 oz (170 ml) ice cubes

1½ oz (45 ml) silver tequila (I recommend Herradura Silver)

½ oz (15 ml) orange liqueur

½ oz (15 ml) agave nectar

1½ oz (45 ml) freshly squeezed lime juice

¼ oz (7 ml) watermelon syrup

GARNISH
Salt for rim of glass
2 watermelon cubes, ½" (13 mm) each

GLASS
Martini

Place the watermelon cubes and habanero ring slice in a cocktail shaker and gently muddle the mixture 2-3 times. Fill the cocktail shaker with ice and top with the tequila, orange liqueur, agave nectar, lime juice and watermelon syrup. Cover the shaker with a tight-fitting lid and shake 12–15 times, until the ice has broken up slightly and the mixture is thoroughly combined.

Place the salt on a flat small plate and gently press the rim of a chilled martini glass into the salt to evenly coat the rim. Strain the margarita into the glass and garnish with 2 cubes of watermelon.

Mojito de Mexico

MEXICAN MOJITO

Mojitos are typically thought of as a Cuban drink, but this rendition adds a Mexican twist by replacing the rum with luscious tequila. It's a perfect way to utilize all of the bright mint that is so abundant in the gardens and at the farmers' markets in the warm summer months.

YIELD: 1 SERVING

---

4 mint sprigs

1 tbsp (12 g) sugar

1 lime, quartered

6 oz (170 ml) ice cubes

1½ oz (45 ml) silver tequila (I recommend Herradura Silver)

2 oz (57 ml) club soda

1 oz (28 ml) lemon-lime soda

GARNISH
Fresh mint sprig

GLASS
Tall glass

Place the mint sprigs and the sugar into a large mixing glass or cocktail shaker. Squeeze the juice from 3 of the lime wedges into the mixing glass and muddle together.

Add the ice and the tequila to the shaker and cover tightly. Shake the glass vigorously 12–15 times, and then pour into a tall glass. Slowly pour the club and lemon-lime sodas into the glass. Garnish with a sprig of mint.

Ramorita

STRAWBERRY LIME MARGARITA

Although I have listed this drink as a strawberry margarita, it is slightly different with the tangy addition of citrusy orange liqueur and fresh lime juice. Nonetheless, it is a refreshing twist on a regular margarita that combines sweet strawberries with my favorite tequila.

YIELD: 1 SERVING

2 strawberries

6 oz (170 ml) ice cubes

1½ oz (45 ml) silver tequila (I recommend Herradura Silver)

½ oz (15 ml) orange liqueur

½ oz (15 ml) agave nectar

1½ oz (45 ml) freshly squeezed lime juice

GARNISH
Strawberry slice

GLASS
Tall glass

Place the strawberries in a cocktail shaker and muddle 5–6 times until the strawberries are coarsely smashed. Fill the cocktail shaker with ice and top with the tequila, orange liqueur, agave nectar and lime juice. Cover the shaker with a tight-fitting lid and shake 12–15 times, until the ice has broken up slightly and the mixture is thoroughly combined.

Strain the drink into a tall glass filled with ice and garnish with a strawberry slice.

El Pepino

CUCUMBER MARGARITA

Fresh cucumbers have a naturally refreshing quality that goes so well with the citrusy flavor of quality silver tequila. In this recipe, the cucumber's crisp, clean flavor adds a surprising twist on the classic margarita.

The addition of jalapeño finishes the drink with a slight hint of spice.

YIELD: 1 SERVING

---

3 cucumber slices

6 oz (170 ml) ice cubes

1½ oz (45 ml) silver tequila (I recommend Herradura Silver)

½ oz (15 ml) orange liqueur

½ oz (15 ml) agave nectar

1½ oz (45 ml) freshly squeezed lime juice

GARNISH
Salt for rim of glass
1 jalapeño slice

GLASS
Short rocks glass

Place the cucumbers in a shaker and gently muddle 6–7 times until they are slightly crushed. Fill a cocktail shaker with ice and top with the tequila, orange liqueur, agave nectar and lime juice. Cover the shaker with a tight-fitting lid and shake 12–15 times, until the ice has broken up slightly and the mixture is thoroughly combined.

Place the salt on a flat small plate and gently press the rim of a chilled rocks glass into the salt to evenly coat the rim. Strain the drink into the glass and garnish with a jalapeño slice.

Margarita de Pomelo

RUBY GRAPEFRUIT MARGARITA

Fresh grapefruit and tequila are an amazing combination, and this recipe is one of my favorite ways to blend the two. The tartness of the grapefruit is perfectly balanced by the sweetness of the agave nectar.

Feel free to replace the salt rim with a mixture of chipotle powder and salt to create a drink with a smoky, spicy kick.

YIELD: 1 SERVING

2 fresh grapefruit segments

6 oz (170 ml) ice cubes

1½ oz (45 ml) silver tequila (I recommend Herradura Silver)

½ oz (15 ml) orange liqueur

1 oz (30 ml) agave nectar

1 oz (30 ml) freshly squeezed lime juice

GARNISH
Salt for rim of glass
1 grapefruit segment

GLASS
Martini or margarita

Place the grapefruit segments in a cocktail shaker and gently muddle 8-10 times until the grapefruit is thoroughly crushed. Fill the cocktail shaker with ice and top with the tequila, orange liqueur, agave nectar and lime juice. Cover the shaker with a tight-fitting lid and shake 12-15 times, until the ice has broken up slightly and the mixture is thoroughly combined.

Place the salt on a flat small plate and gently press the rim of a chilled martini glass into the salt to coat the rim. Strain the margarita into the glass and garnish with an additional grapefruit segment.

Margarita de Arandano y Salvia

CRANBERRY SAGE MARGARITA

Cranberries are not typically found in Mexican cooking, but their flavor enhances the equally tart citrus taste of limes so well it is a shame that they are not used more often. This drink makes an elegant way to combine the traditional flavors of New England with the vibrant flavors of Mexico for the perfect drink for the holidays or any other gathering.

YIELD: 1 SERVING

---

6 oz (170 ml) ice cubes

1½ oz (45 ml) silver tequila (I recommend Herradura Silver)

½ oz (15 ml) orange liqueur

½ oz (15 ml) agave nectar

1½ oz (45 ml) freshly squeezed lime juice

6 fresh sage leaves

1 oz (30 ml) cranberry puree, store-bought or freshly made (recipe follows)

GARNISH
Sugar for rim of glass
3 fresh cranberries
1 fresh sage leaf

GLASS
Martini

Fill a cocktail shaker with ice and top with the tequila, orange liqueur, agave nectar, lime juice, sage leaves and cranberry puree. Cover the shaker with a tight-fitting lid and shake 12–15 times, until the ice has broken up slightly and the mixture is thoroughly combined.

Place the sugar on a flat small plate and gently press the rim of a chilled martini glass into the sugar to evenly coat the rim. Strain the margarita into the glass and garnish with the fresh cranberries and a sage leaf.

Puree de Arandanos

CRANBERRY PUREE

This is a quick puree that is essential in the Cranberry Sage Margarita (above). The mixture should be very smooth and have the thickness of a runny milkshake. Add water if necessary to reach the correct consistency.

YIELD: 3 CUPS (500 ML)

½ cup (120 ml) freshly squeezed orange juice

½ cup (96 g) sugar

8 oz (227 g) fresh cranberries

Stir together the orange juice and sugar in a medium-size saucepan and heat over medium heat for 5 minutes, until the sugar has completely melted. Stir in the cranberries and continue to cook for an additional 5–10 minutes, stirring frequently, until the cranberries burst.

Remove the mixture from the heat and let cool slightly. Once cool, puree the mixture in a blender for 2 minutes and strain through a medium-mesh strainer, discarding the large particles. Refrigerate until needed.

Sangrita de Mexico

NOT-SO-CLASSIC MEXICAN SANGRITA

Sangrita is a traditional Mexican drink served as a chaser when drinking high-end tequilas. At the restaurants, we serve it with our tequila samplings.

In Mexico, you can buy various versions served in cans, but they can be heavy on the lime flavor. My chef de cuisine, Matt, developed this recipe that encompasses all of the best qualities of sangrita: tartness, bold flavor, brininess and, of course, a small hint of spice.

It's fantastic on its own, but drink while sipping tequila for the perfect palate cleanser.

YIELD: 4 SERVINGS

6 Roma tomatoes, dry roasted (page 18)

12 tomatillos, peeled and dry roasted (page 18)

6 garlic cloves, dry roasted and peeled (page 18)

½ fresh habanero chile, dry roasted and stemmed (page 18)

¼ cup (59 ml) Worcestershire sauce

1 tbsp (15 g) celery salt

3 tbsp (45 g) dark chile powder

2 celery stalks

Salt to taste

GLASS
Shot glass

Place all of the ingredients in a blender and puree, in batches if necessary, until extremely smooth. Strain through a small-mesh strainer and discard the large particles. Serve in a shot glass and sip along with your favorite tequila.

Agua Fresca

MEXICAN STRAWBERRY LIME WATER

If you've ever visited Mexico, you've most likely witnessed street vendors selling large glass jugs of assorted nonalcoholic juices, or agua fresca (fresh water). This is just one of the many refreshing flavors that is available. It makes a delicious thirst-quencher and leftovers can be used to make your own frozen Mexican popsicles, paletas.

YIELD: 2-3 SERVINGS

½ cup (96 g) sugar

¼ tsp salt

3 cups (710 ml) water

6 cups (910 g) sliced fresh strawberries

1 cup (240 ml) freshly squeezed lime juice

Ice

GARNISH
Fresh mint

GLASS
Rocks glass

Combine the sugar, salt and water in a medium-size saucepan and heat over medium-low heat until the sugar and salt have completely dissolved. Set aside to cool.

Combine 3 cups (454 g) of the sliced strawberries with 1½ cups (355 ml) of the cooled sugar-water mixture in a blender and puree until extremely smooth. Once completely blended, pour the mixture into a large glass pitcher along with the remaining 3 cups (454 g) strawberries and 1½ cups (355 ml) water mixture.

Stir in the lime juice and ice. Ladle into individual glasses and garnish with a fresh mint sprig.

Tequila Vieja Moda

TEQUILA OLD FASHIONED

Aged tequila has a rich, smooth flavor that is amazing sipped by itself, but this drink is an excellent option if you are looking to intensify its flavor. Tequila Vieja Moda is one of my favorite drinks.

YIELD: 1 SERVING

¼ oz agave nectar

1 dash bitters

1-2 inch (2.5-5 cm) strip orange peel, orange portion only

2 oz (60 ml) tequila (I recommend Herradura Anejo)

3 oz (90 ml) ice cubes

GARNISH
Cherry

GLASS
Old fashioned

Place the agave nectar, bitters and orange peel in an old fashioned glass and lightly muddle. Place the tequila and ice cubes in the glass and gently stir. Garnish with a cherry and serve.

Cocoa de Mexicano

MEXICAN-SPICED HOT CHOCOLATE

What could possibly improve decadent hot chocolate spiced with Mexican chocolate and cinnamon? A dash of chipotle powder, of course.

YIELD: 2 SERVINGS

---

2 cups (473 ml) whole milk

2 (6" [15 cm]) cinnamon sticks, preferably Mexican

6 oz (170 g) Mexican chocolate, chopped into small pieces

GARNISH
Chipotle chile powder
Cinnamon sticks

GLASS
Mugs

Place the milk and cinnamon sticks in a medium-size saucepan and bring just to a simmer over low heat. Be careful not to let the milk come to a full boil. Remove the milk from the heat and using a slotted spoon, remove and discard the cinnamon sticks. Slowly whisk in the chocolate until it has completely melted.

Pour the hot chocolate into individual mugs and garnish with a whole cinnamon stick and a dash of chipotle chile powder.

Note: Mexican chocolate is now readily available and can be found in the Latin section of most grocery stores.

Café de Olla

MEXICAN CLAY POT COFFEE

In Mexico, café de olla is often made with eggshells; however, my version strays away from tradition and omits the shells, but not the flavor. If you love coffee, you'll love this spiced version. It combines bold spices such as anise and cloves with sweet Mexican sugar and tart orange peel. It's a tradition to make this coffee every holiday morning, but admittedly, it is so good that I sometimes can't wait and make it a little more often.

YIELD: 4 SERVINGS

---

1 qt (1 L) water

2 whole cloves

1 (6" [15 cm]) cinnamon stick, preferably Mexican

2 star anise, whole

3 oz (85 g) piloncilla or 3 oz (85 g) light brown sugar

Peel from ½ orange

6 tbsp (34 g) ground coffee

GLASS
Mugs

Place the water, cloves, cinnamon stick, star anise and piloncilla in a large saucepan or clay pot and bring to a simmer over low heat. Simmer the mixture for 2 minutes, stirring frequently, until the piloncilla has completely dissolved.

Remove the mixture from the heat and stir in the orange peel and coffee. Allow the coffee to steep for 4 minutes. Strain the mixture through a fine-mesh strainer or coffee filter and serve.

Menús Sugeridos
SUGGESTED MENUS

Taste of Yucatán

Not-So-Classic Mexican Sangrita (page 186)

Fiery Habanero Salsa (page 165)

Fresh Corn Tortillas (page 21)

Yucatán Achiote Seasoned Pork (page 66)

Yucatán Pickled Red Onions (page 120)

Refried Black Beans (page 126)

Christmas Eve Open House

Cranberry Sage Margarita (page 185)

Roasted Oaxacan-Spiced Orange and Butternut Squash Soup (page 108)

Red Chile Pork Tamales (page 41)

Roasted Pork Leg in Adobo Sauce (page 64)

Lime Tarts with Ancho Graham Crust and Agave Whipped Cream (page 143)

New Year's Dinner

Tequila Old Fashioned (page 189)

Ancho-Glazed Chicken Empanadas (page 38)

Corn, Poblano and Lobster Bisque (page 111)

Pumpkin Seed–Crusted Rack of Lamb with Oaxacan Red Mole Sauce (page 74)

Classic Mexican Vanilla Flan (page 135)

Summer Fiesta

Watermelon Habanero Margarita (page 176)

Fresh Avocado Guacamole (page 169)

Mezcal-Braised Spare Ribs with Spicy Chipotle Molasses Sauce (page 63)

Mexican Grilled Corn (page 124)

Flourless Chocolate Ancho Cake (page 136)

Seaside Grilling Party

Classic Zapoteca Margarita (page 175)

Grilled Mexican Caeser Salad with Poblano-Pumpkin Seed Dressing (page 115)

Red Chile–Grilled Whole Fish (page 97)

Grilled Bananas with Sea Salt and Rum Ice Cream (page 140)

Sunset Cocktail Party

Mexican Strawberry Lime Water (page 189)

Ruby Grapefruit Margarita (page 182)

Mexican Mojito (page 179)

Tequila Old Fashion (page 189)

Pistachio and Goat Cheese Guacamole (page 170)

Crisp Corn Masa "Sandals" with Fragrant Mushrooms (page 34)

Sweet Corn Ice Cream with Salted Caramel Corn (page 148)

Mail - Order Sources

THE CHILE GUY

www.thechileguy.com

Whole chile pods

D'ARTAGNAN

www.dartagnan.com

Duck, specialty meat and duck fat

GRYFFON RIDGE SPICE MERCHANTS

http://gryffonridge.com

Spices

MELISSA GUERRA LATIN KITCHEN MARKET

www.melissaguerra.com

Mexican cooking equipment and tableware

MEXGROCER.COM

www.mexgrocer.com

Mexican chocolate, spices and miscellaneous

MOZZARELLA COMPANY

www.mozzco.com

Specialty Mexican cheese

SEA SALT LOBSTER COMPANY

www.seasaltlobster.com

Lobster

Acknowledgments

My family, for all of the love, faith and sacrifices you make in helping me follow my dreams and for making my dreams our dreams. For being my shining, smiling light at the end of the tunnel and end of long workdays that seem to go on and on. This book and my life wouldn't have been possible without you.

My father, for teaching me a love of the land and that hard work only makes the end result more rewarding.

My partners and dear friends in the restaurants and the kitchen. Tom, Matt, Sergio—you are the backbone, and words cannot express the gratitude I have for simply having all of you in my life.

My restaurant team at Zapoteca and Mixteca, whether you are with me now or have moved on to the next chapter in your life. Thank you for your passion and dedication.

Ted Axelrod, my photographer, whose patience and determination played such a key role in all aspects of this book, not just the beautiful images, and whose insane humor made me laugh at times when laughing seemed almost impossible.

Angie Helton, my PR agent, for your friendship and all of your hard work that often went far beyond the call of duty.

My mentors, Chefs Illiana de la Vega and Phyllis Flaherty, for further igniting my passion for Mexican cuisine and culture and for making me always want to do better.

The amazing team at Page Street Publishing, for believing in me and allowing me to fulfill a lifelong dream and check one thing off of my bucket list, and for your incredible amount of knowledge, creativity, humor and unbelievable patience.

Those who dream of a career in the culinary world—follow your heart and chase your dreams. You can do it.

My amazing friends. Writing a cookbook is never a solo effort, and your support, feedback and friendship were essential to me every step of the way.

About the Author

SHANNON BARD is the executive chef and co-owner of two nationally acclaimed contemporary Mexican restaurants in New England (Zapoteca Restaurante Y Tequileria and Mixteca Taqueria Y Cantina). Although she began cooking at a very early age, she did not venture into a career as a professional chef until later in life following a successful career as a stay-at-home mom. Because of this, she brings a unique perspective to the professional cooking scene as well as your home kitchen.

She has traveled extensively, working with some of the finest chefs in the world, and brought back a contemporary menu that showcases her unique, bold interpretation of traditional Mexican cuisine.

Shannon has been honored by the James Beard Foundation with an invitation to cook at the prestigious James Beard House and has appeared on numerous Food Network series, including *Beat Bobby Flay* and *The Kitchen Inferno*. Her work has been featured in *Bon Appetit Magazine*, *The Wall Street Journal*, Fox.com, *Bella Magazine*, *Food Network Magazine*, *Maine Magazine*, *DownEast Magazine*, *New Hampshire Magazine*, *Portland Magazine*, *Old Port Magazine*, *The Latin Kitchen* and many, many more.

In *The Gourmet Mexican Kitchen—A Cookbook*, Shannon reveals some her secrets for creating bold Mexican flavors in your home kitchen and the art of using simple, traditional Mexican techniques to create truly memorable dishes.

She currently lives in Kennebunk, Maine, with her husband and four children.

Index